NEW YORK CITY
Trolleys
In Color

by William D. Volkmer

Copyright © 2002
Morning Sun Books, Inc.

All rights reserved. This book may not be reproduced in part or in whole without written permission from the publisher, except in the case of brief quotations or reproductions of the cover for the purposes of review.

Library of Congress
Catalog Card No.2002103682

First Printing
ISBN 1-58248-081-8

Published by
Morning Sun Books, Inc.
9 Pheasant Lane
Scotch Plains, NJ 07076
Printed in Korea

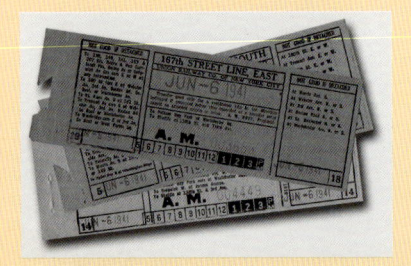

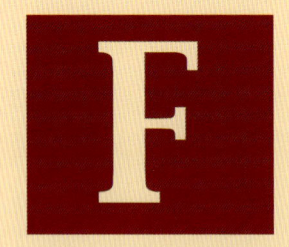

Robert J. Yanosey, President
To access our full library *In Color* visit us at
www.morningsunbooks.com

Foreword

As an amateur pianist, I once asked a professional musician if he could teach me how to imitate the country piano technique used by the real pros Floyd Cramer, Charlie Rich and a few others. I will never forget his answer. "Son, it helps if you were born in Tennessee."

Having done *some* of the research necessary to do any book on the subject of rail transit in New York City, I will be the first to say, "It not only *helps* if you were born in New York, it must be mandatory!" Without the tremendous help from native New Yorker, and Electric Railroaders' Association scion, Karl Groh, the chances of this book being error free would have been somewhat less than zero. With Karl's patient answering of my "dumb question of the day", his supply of ERA reading material, and painstaking study of the slides, I hope this book will be of passing interest to New Yorkers as well as those who have never been near the "Big Apple." As a close second following Karl would be Don Harold, who filled in the Brooklyn voids. Whereas Karl's main strength is the Bronx area, Don was able to obtain parts of the collection of the late Everett A. White, one of the men instrumental in preserving some of the Brooklyn cars for posterity.

My thanks also go to publisher Bob Yanosey, who ferreted out several slide collections upon which to draw from, including collections of Edward S. Miller, Frank Pfhuler, Al Holtz, R. Fillman, Walter Zullig, Charlie Ballard, the Lawson K. Hill Collection, now the property of the Boston Chapter, N.R.H.S., the Eugene Van Dusen Collection, and the late James J. Buckley photos, courtesy of P. Allen Copeland. Karl frequently drew upon the knowledge and help of Donald Harold and Bernie Linder, both of New York, to fill in the few voids in his amazingly factual memory. Don proved to be our important link to the trolley bus information, when needed. This information was also aided and abetted by Bernie Linder.

By far the single most valuable *printed* resource used in preparing this book was a publication put out in 1953 by Vincent J. Seyfried called "Third Avenue Railway Roster of Equipment, 1853-1953. I consider this book, as many others do, to be the Bible on Third Avenue Railway surface equipment. Vincent F. Seyfried, literally and figuratively is "The Man that Wrote the Book" on the Third Avenue Railway.

Any mistakes found in this book are mine and definitely not his or Karl's. Even Karl managed to learn a few things he never knew, while doing the research. And that is saying something. Another unsung hero of the New York trolley history scene is Edward B. Watson who compiled the most factual data on Brooklyn streetcar operation.

As a special thank you, I wish to dedicate this book to Karl Groh, a truly dedicated New York historian.

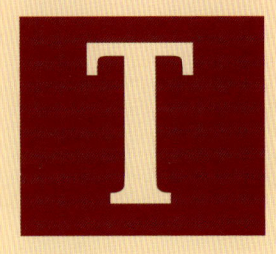

Table of Contents

Third Avenue Railway 4-43
Brooklyn and Queens Transit 44-111
South Brooklyn Railway 112-115
Queensborough Bridge Railway 116-125
Preserved Cars of New York City . . .126-128

Introduction
NEW YORK CITY

GIVE MY REGARDS TO BROADWAY; REMEMBER ME TO HERALD SQUARE. EAST SIDE, WEST SIDE, ALL AROUND THE TOWN, NEW YORK, NEW YORK, IT'S A WONDERFUL TOWN.

There have been dozens of songs written about New York. There have been dozens of books written about the subways, the elevateds, and yes, the streetcars. The magazine articles dealing with various facets of New York transit are legion in number. It would be a virtual impossibility to put between any two covers a complete history of the entire system, because unlike most city systems, in New York there were and still are, major changes occurring just about every time the sun rises over the East River. As we found out in doing the small amount of research necessary to put together a photo synopsis of the thirteen year period from 1943 to 1956, New York transit history is like basket weave that dates back to the 1860s, when steam train lines began hauling passengers to the beaches at Coney Island.

New York had steam-drawn elevated railways in the late 1870s. These lines were already twenty years old when Frank J. Sprague figured out how to electrify and operate the trains as multiple-unit consists. Gradually, the steam roads in Brooklyn were converted to high-platform elevated trains, operating on the surface with trolley poles for current pickup in contrast to the third rail being used on the Manhattan side of the East River. As the city's population expanded, some of the surface lines were put up on elevated trackage above the city streets, while lighter patronage lines reverted to streetcar operation.

Just to give the reader a sampling of how rapid and how often the transit picture changes in New York, let us set our calendar to the year 1936, the year of PCC car introduction to Brooklyn, and, indeed, to the nation. For over forty years, Brooklyn had averaged 125 new streetcars *per year* onto its streets. Third Avenue Railway shops were building two new streetcars *per week*. Fast forward now, to 1956. The 1938-era Third Avenue cars had already been sold off to foreign countries for almost ten years. No additional PCC cars had been added, and even the nine-year-old trolley coach fleet was in rapid decline. Numerous generations of gas and diesel buses had come and gone from the scene.

Space limitations here prevent us from going into much of the detail, but historians of New York City transit need not look far to find even the most minute track change or car modification chronicled in detail by the New York-based Electric Railroaders' Association publications, most notably, their magazine, "Headlights", as well as the New York Division "Bulletin."

Since the oldest color slides that we were able to locate dated back to 1942 and the last trolley operated on the Queensborough Bridge Railway in 1957; we are forced to limit the scope of this book to that fourteen-year period. Brooklyn operated trolley coaches (called "electric buses" in Brooklyn) until 1960 so we are allowed to stretch the fourteen-year coverage to eighteen by including this mode of transportation.

N Y C

1

Third Avenue Railway System

■■■ Manhattan, Bronx, Yonkers, and Westchester County ■■■

Horse cars began operating on October 8, 1853 in what is now mid-town Manhattan, 65th Street and 3rd Avenue to Ann Street and Park Row. Gradually, the horse system expanded and clearly a better means of propulsion was needed. So in 1884-85, a cable car system was tested on Amsterdam Avenue. In 1886, a second cable car line opened on 125th Street. In 1893, Third Avenue itself was converted to cable cars. Two years later, in 1895 they finally joined the world of electrified transit, and 1899 had converted all of the cable lines to electric-powered cars. Trolleys, in the case of the Third Avenue might technically be a misnomer, because the Manhattan routes were uniformly all powered by an underground conduit in the center of the track gauge. A paddle under the car (always referred to in New York as a "plow") followed the conduit, collecting current to power the cars and returning the current via a second rail inside the conduit. Washington, D.C., Paris, France, and London, England were the only other streetcar operations known to have used this method of current collection.

Abandonment of the lighter patronage lines in Westchester County began in 1924 with bus substitution in New Rochelle, and conversion to bus gained momentum during the 1930s. Mainstay of the car fleet in the 1920s and early 1930s was a group of more than 400 convertible and other wooden cars built by Brill from 1908 to 1912. However, the Third Avenue management made the conscious decision in 1933 to retain their heaviest car lines and extensively modernize them in a manner apart from the practice of most other large cities that had reached this same conclusion. Whereas the other cities had banded together to form the "Presidents' Conference Committee" (PCC), Third Avenue opted to go it alone and shun the PCC streamliners.

They first purchased as many late-model pre-owned streetcars as they were able to find, and extensively rebuilt them prior to putting them into service in New York. All of these cars were assigned to lines in the Bronx operating out of Kingsbridge Carhouse. In common with Allentown, PA, Birmingham, AL, Atlanta, GA, and Norfolk, VA to name a few, Third Avenue purchased quantities of cars from San Antonio, TX, Staten Island, NY, Kankakee, IL, Ironwood, MI, Eau Claire, WI, Attleboro, MA, Hartford, CT, Andrescoggin and Kennebec, (ME), and Sunbury & Selinsgrove, PA. After all the second hand cars were obtained, the company began manufacturing a substantial fleet of new cars in their 65th St. shops in Manhattan.

In 1934-35 ninety-nine cars were constructed by stretching old Third Avenue single truck cars, in order to make a larger-capacity, double truck car. These became the 100 series cars on the Third Avenue, many of which operated right up until the last day of service in 1952. One additional "recycled streetcar" on the Third Avenue roster was car 1259 which was renumbered from 1605, making an even 100 re-cycled streetcars, a term practiced by Third Avenue long before the word became popular in the vernacular. Cars 102-200 were known as the "stretched" cars, and car 101 was not constructed until the conclusion of the program. It was built as a prototype for the then proposed new 300 series cars that were built new, from scratch, immediately thereafter. Car 101 was unique in that it had skirts under the bumpers, giving it a dressy effect, not repeated until the Huffliners and the higher numbered 600 series cars were built.

In 1936, a second set of cars very similar to the 100 series was constructed, numbered 301-400. Many cars in this series were also still in service on the last day of Third Avenue Railway operation in Yonkers, on November 8, 1952.

The perceived need for a front entrance, center exit Peter Witt design car (similar to the PCC) prompted the company under its President at the time, S.W. Huff, to construct 75 such cars (551-625) called "Huffliners" by the locals. The idea of center-exit on streetcars in New York did not seem to work well, the fact not withstanding that it seemed to work on thousands of buses in the area. So the idea was not duplicated in future car projects on the Third Avenue. These cars were all subsequently sold to Sao Paulo, Brazil following abandonment of the Manhattan lines. Only one car in this series (551) ever sported a trolley pole. That car had poles only briefly for testing purposes in Mt. Vernon. In Brazil, the cars of course had trolley poles and many were converted to single end operation. While in Brazil, they were numbered in the 1700s.

The last group of new cars to be constructed in the Third Avenue 65th Street shops was 60 cars, fairly identical to the 300 series (626-685). Their design reverted to the time-tested front entrance, rear-exit design. All but the first two of this group (plus the five described below) had "rubber sandwich" wheels, similar in design to the PCC cars, for noise reduction purposes. The 626-645 were built in 1938 and 1939 without trolley poles and were used primarily on the X- 59th Street Crosstown line. On Sundays they could also be found operating on 42nd Street. When the 59th Street line was motorized (it was the first of the Crosstown lines to go), the cars were re-assigned to the T-3rd Avenue-Amsterdam route. The 646 to 685 series were equipped with trolley poles, and were initially used only on the S- Southern Boulevard and T- Tremont lines in the Bronx. Following abandonment of the Bronx lines, in August 1948, 42 of this group were sold to Vienna, Austria and 15 to Bombay, India. Three of the Vienna cars have been returned to the United States for preservation and a fourth resides in the National Tramway museum in Crich, England. One additional car was preserved in Graz, Austria, and one in Brussels, Belguim.

As an aside, it should be noted that five cars in this series, numbers 651 to 655 originally had regular Brill 77E trucks installed because they were leased to the Queensborough Bridge Railway. This was done while the Steinway lines (originally Manhattan Bridge 3-cent line) cars were in the 65th Street Shop being rebuilt for further bridge service. The always thrifty Third Avenue company felt that silent trucks would be a waste of money on cars that operated 90% of their time on bridges. They were later assigned to the T- Tremont Avenue line in the Bronx without a change of trucks. Because these cars always had Brill 77E trucks, the car that is currently at Seashore Museum is so equipped. The car preserved at Branford has the rubber sandwich trucks.

The PCC as a streetcar concept was never adopted by Third Avenue Railway and, as the 1930s era cars became obsolete, bus substitution on all lines became the norm until the very last red and yellow streetcar operated. Sometime around 1943, in deference to the substantial increase in the use of motorbuses, the official company name was changed to Third Avenue Transit System and a small circular emblem replaced the spelled out lettering on the sides of the cars.

This photo typifies the equipment used on the Third Avenue Transit System during the later days following abandonment of the Bronx routes. There were approximately 250 cars of similar design. This view shows car 308 at the end of the Nepperhan Avenue line in Yonkers with the obligatory pose by the motorman.
(Steve Bogen)

Manhattan Lines

In the 1930s and 1940s there were seven rail lines remaining in operation covering Manhattan Island from tip to tip. All lines were underground-conduit-powered, as the use of overhead trolley wire had been banned in Manhattan early in the 20th century. An exception to this rule was a variance that allowed short extensions of Bronx lines to enter Manhattan under wires on 135th St., 155th St., 181st St. and 207th St.

The long T-3rd & Amsterdam Avenues route began opposite City Hall in lower Manhattan, proceeded up Third Avenue underneath the elevated structure until it reached 125th Street. There it turned left on 125th Street sharing trackage with the 125th Street Crosstown line as well as the K- Broadway Kingsbridge line as far as 162nd St. and Amsterdam Ave. At that point the Kingsbridge turned left and the T line continued straight to its 190th Street terminus. It was converted to bus on May 7, 1947.

There were three crosstown lines; all designated "X" on the dash sign. "X" was a Third Avenue-universal symbol for "crosstown", with but one exception. In the Bronx there were two Crosstown lines that shared the same street (181st in Manhattan) for a short distance. That 181st St. route, which followed Tremont and 180th Street in the Bronx, was dubbed the "Z" Crosstown line.

The 59th Street Crosstown line was abandoned November 10, 1946. The 42nd Street Crosstown was abandoned five days later, on November 15, 1946, and the 125th Street line was abandoned July 1, 1947.

Another long Manhattan route, served in the latter years exclusively by Huffliners, was the B- Broadway line. This route began on 42nd Street at First Avenue, and operated west on 42nd Street to Seventh Avenue. At Times Square it veered to the left on Broadway and ran north on Broadway to 125th Street where it turned right, and then a quick left onto Amsterdam Avenue for four blocks, terminating at the 129th Street and Amsterdam Avenue carhouse. This line was abandoned December 14, 1946.

Line K- Kingsbridge operated from Third Avenue and 125th Street west on 125th Street to Amsterdam Avenue. It went north on Amsterdam to 162nd where it turned left onto St. Nicholas joining Broadway at 168th St. From 168th and Broadway, it ran north to 225th Street in the Bronx, where it turned back. The last seven blocks of this line operated under trolley wire in Manhattan because this trackage was also used by Bronx cars accessing the Kingsbridge Carhouse, at 218th and Broadway. The K line was exclusively served by Huffliners during the last year from December 15, 1946 until its abandonment on June 28, 1947.

One other Manhattan line was the 10- Tenth Avenue line that ran from ferry slip at 42nd Street and Twelfth Avenue north on Tenth Avenue to 71st Street where it joined Broadway for the run past Columbia University, to 125th Street and 12th Avenue which was the Fort Lee Ferry terminal. Last day for the number 10 line was November 16, 1946.

Third Avenue 564 northbound on 7th Ave. at 42nd St. (Times Square) May 30, 1942.
(Lawson Hill, Boston Chapter, NHRS Collection)

BRONX LINES

There were a total of seventeen streetcar lines operating in the Bronx during the 1940s. Four of these routes carried the ubiquitous "X" on the dasher signifying that they were "Crosstown" lines. Bronx crosstown lines operated over 138th, 149th, 163rd, and 180th Streets. The 180th Street crosstown carried the letter "Z", because it shared a short length of trackage with the X- 167th Street line at their western terminal on 181st St. at Broadway in Manhattan. Other routes operating streetcars in the Bronx were A- Westchester Ave., B- Bailey Ave., B- Boston Road, C- Bronx-Van Cortlandt Parks Crosstown, L- St. Anns Ave., O- Ogden Ave., S- Sedgwick Ave., S- Southern Boulevard, T- Tremont Ave., U- University Ave., V- Williamsbridge, and W- Webster and White Plains Ave.

From this list, it can be readily seen that Third Avenue Railway had no aversion to having two routes with the same alpha designator! Other than a handful of lightly patronized routes that were discontinued around World War I, the Third Avenue Bronx operation was largely still intact at the time wholesale bus conversion took place, between March 1947 and August 1948. The final five car lines were converted on August 21, 1948.

WESTCHESTER COUNTY LINES

Mount Vernon, New Rochelle, and the area around Pelham Bay were served by fifteen Third Avenue Railway routes, all but two of which were abandoned in between 1926 and 1939. The two surviving lines lasted until December 17, 1950, because they were basically feeder lines to the New York subway system and hence, heavily patronized to the end. These two lines were the A-Main Street, New Rochelle, and the B- Mt. Vernon R.R. station to subway, via White Plains Avenue. The predecessor operator of these lines was the Westchester Electric Railroad and title had passed to the Third Avenue Railway via the Union Railway management. The trackage of the B line in the vicinity of Mt. Vernon R.R. station including the terminal point was shared with Yonkers' 7- Yonkers Avenue line, the very last Third Avenue line to be abandoned, November 8, 1952.

YONKERS LINES

Yonkers is New York State's third largest city, behind New York and Buffalo. Yet, in 1951, when the author first visited it with camera in hand, it was one of the last six remaining small city streetcar operations in the entire United States. The other five were Atlantic City, NJ, Scranton, PA, Altoona, PA, Washington, PA and Johnstown, PA.

Yonkers, in 1951-52 was truly a railfan's paradise, with seven distinct car lines comprised of 26 1/2 miles in Yonkers (Westchester County) and 2 1/2 miles inside the Bronx, wandering into and out of downtown Yonkers. Five of the seven lines originated adjacent to the New York Central passenger station at the foot of Main Street. In the early 1950s the system carried about 60,000 passengers per day.

There was a three-story carbarn complete with a trolley elevator to house the remaining 89 streetcars, assorted snow sweepers and other work equipment. Nearly all of the streets in downtown Yonkers were paved in cobblestones and with the constant hum of traction motors and steel wheels a-grinding and squealing, the town was a delight to visit. I visited there on three occasions, riding, among others, the Nepperhan Avenue line, which was side of the road, single track, with passing sidings operation. Unfortunately I had not yet graduated into color photography in those days so I was extremely pleased to be able to use Jim Buckley and others' color work to illustrate this portion of the book.

My third visit, and last, visit to Yonkers was on November 2, 1952. Unfortunately I was a day too late, because all of the lines but one had been abandoned by the previous day. Inside the barn, a wrecking crew was in the process of dismantling car 194. Someone had chalked on its flanks "last streetcar to operate in the Bronx." So, I asked if I could have the controller handle from that particular car. I still have it in my collection.

Together with lines 2 and 3, line 1- Broadway-Warburton Ave. was considered to be the "Main Line" of Yonkers. Beginning at 242nd Street and Broadway, just below the northern city limits of New York, the line ran north on South Broadway to Getty Square in downtown Yonkers, where it turned left on Main Street running about three blocks. It then turned right onto Warburton Ave. where it operated mostly on single track along the Hudson River palisades to the Yonkers City limits.

Line 2- Broadway – Park Ave., like line 1, connected with the Bronx subway line at 242nd Street and Broadway. Prior to January 24, 1948, Bronx line C shared the tracks a short distance north to the New York City limits, where the C cars turned back. After passing Getty Square in Yonkers, the 2- Park Avenue cars (which alternated with the Warburton Ave. cars) operated up Palisade and Park Avenues. There were a couple of steep hills with manual derails on this line. It was abandoned on November 2, 1952.

Line 3 was a short turn operation of the 1 and 2 lines operating between the Foot of Main Street in Yonkers down to the subway terminal at 242nd Street and Broadway. The line operated on weekends as well when patronage was heavy from Yonkers to the Subway but lighter on the 1 and 2 lines. The last car to operate on this line, the aforementioned car 194, arrived at the foot of Main Street at 6:30 AM November 2, 1952. A scant five hours later it was in the process of being scrapped inside the carbarn.

Line 4- McLean Avenue connected Yonkers with the Jerome Ave. subway line on the east side of Woodlawn Cemetery. Beginning at the elevated station, it operated north a short distance on Central Park Avenue to McLean, where it turned left over to Broadway. It shared Broadway with lines 1, 2, and 3 for a short distance before diverging at New Main Street and crossed Getty Square on Main Street from the east. It too terminated at the carbarn at the foot of Main Street. It was converted to bus on November 1, 1952.

The 5- Nepperhan Avenue line originated at the foot of Main Street, Yonkers and operated on Main to Getty Square where it turned left into Palisade Avenue. It split from the 2 line at Elm and turned left from Elm onto Nepperhan where the line became a single track. After two passing sidings the line continued on the side of the road right-of-way to its northern terminal at Tompkins Avenue. It was abandoned on October 25, 1952.

The 6- Tuckahoe line paralleled the 5 on Saw Mill Road, ending at the New York Central Putnam Division Nepperhan Station on Tuckahoe Road. It too was abandoned on October 25, 1952.

Line 7- Yonkers Avenue proved to be the very last survivor of the once vast Third Avenue Railways system, outlasting the others by only one week. It ran due east from the downtown area along

Yonkers Avenue past Yonkers Raceway and terminated at the Mt. Vernon station of the New Haven Railroad. Conversion of this line to bus on November 9, 1952 completed the motorization of the entire Third Avenue Railway System.

Line 8- Riverdale Avenue was a short two-car shuttle operation on Riverdale Avenue. In prior years before the routes were numbered, this line was through-routed with McLean Avenue, but light riding on Riverdale reduced it to shuttle car statues with only two cars needed. It was single track throughout with but one passing siding on the line. For some reason, the line terminated at Main Street, but did not run east the last several blocks to reach the downtown area. Riverdale was abandoned along with Nepperhan and Tuckahoe on October 25, 1952.

Line 9 - Elm-Walnut, in common with lines 3,4,5,6, and 7 originated at the foot of Main Street opposite the New York Central railroad station and the U.S. Post Office. It operated east on Main St. past Getty Square, over Elm and turned back on Walnut at Yonkers Ave. Being the lightest line on the system, it was abandoned without replacement on October 25, 1952.

Third Avenue crane car #7 at Mt. Vernon Yard in 1947.
(Robert Fillman)

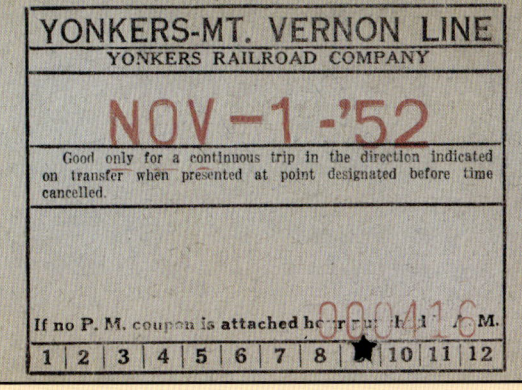

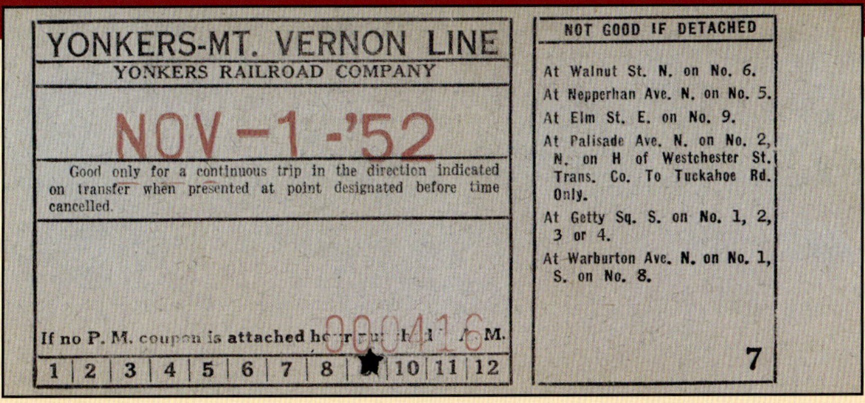

Cars 332 and 359 are at the trolley terminal on 242nd St. at Van Cortland Park. May 20, 1951. This photo graphically illustrates that not only did both lines share the street and terminal, but they managed to arrive in an alternating pattern thanks to carefully scheduling and schedule keeping.
(Eugene Van Dusen)

8 *1-2-3 Broadway in Yonkers*

Looking south at 242nd Street and Broadway, July 12, 1952 we see car 342, one of the "newer" cars still in operation at that late date. *(James J. Buckley, P. Allen Copeland Collection)*

1
B'WAY-WARBURTON

We shall begin our photographic tour of the New York area in the far northwestern corner, Yonkers. The mainstays of the nine Yonkers trolley routes were the three that operated over Broadway between the New York City line at 242nd and Broadway past Getty Square in Yonkers and branching out in three directions to the northern suburbs of Yonkers.

Line 1 went north to Hastings on the Hudson via Warburton Ave. while line 2 went north on Park Ave. Line 3 was a rush hour shuttle between the Foot of Main Street and the subway to relieve the crush loading on the cars.

The three lines were abandoned on November 1, 1952 the next-to-last lines to go.

A view of Main Street, Yonkers on May 20, 1951 shows car 379 southbound (though temporarily heading east) approaching Getty Square. A scene similar to this once inspired artist Norman Rockwell to paint a cover illustration for the *Saturday Evening Post* magazine, showing a lady attempting to park her car, while delaying the streetcar. In Rockwell's inimitable fashion he showed the passengers in the streetcar with their noses pressed against the windshield, watching the action. *(Eugene Van Dusen)*

Southbound car 397 is on Broadway leaving Getty Square on July 12, 1952. This location afforded the traction afficianado a huge amount of streetcar action, even in a time when seemingly every city in the nation had already converted to all bus operation. *(Lawson K. Hill, Boston Chapter, NRHS Collection)*

10 *1-2-3 Broadway in Yonkers*

1-2-3 Broadway in Yonkers

(Right) In this view car 332 is shown at the same location, 242nd St. and Broadway IRT Station. However the camera points in the opposite direction showing the staircase from which the shot above was made. The date is May 20, 1951.
 (Eugene Van Dusen)

1-2-3 Broadway in Yonkers

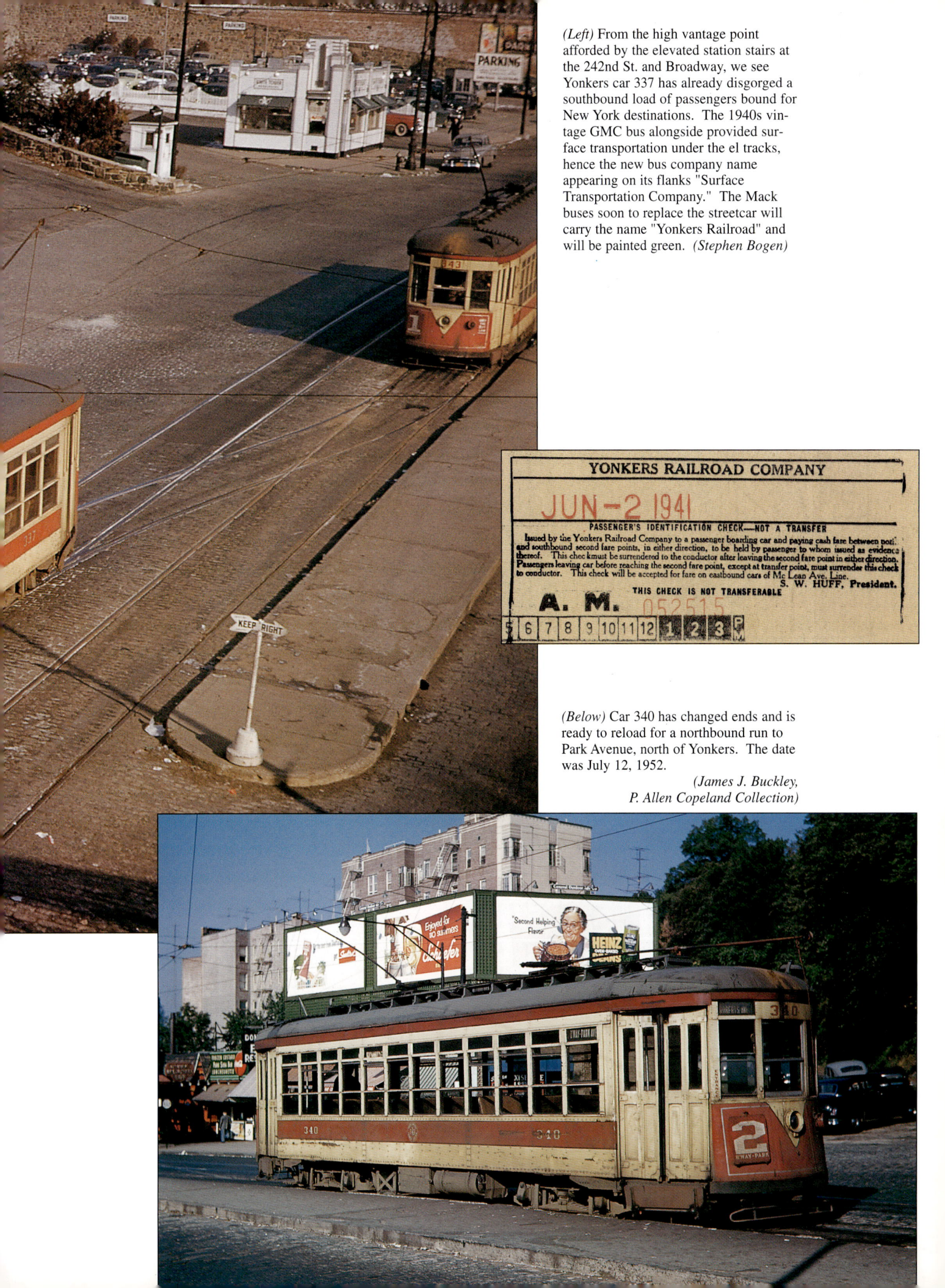

(Left) From the high vantage point afforded by the elevated station stairs at the 242nd St. and Broadway, we see Yonkers car 337 has already disgorged a southbound load of passengers bound for New York destinations. The 1940s vintage GMC bus alongside provided surface transportation under the el tracks, hence the new bus company name appearing on its flanks "Surface Transportation Company." The Mack buses soon to replace the streetcar will carry the name "Yonkers Railroad" and will be painted green. *(Stephen Bogen)*

(Below) Car 340 has changed ends and is ready to reload for a northbound run to Park Avenue, north of Yonkers. The date was July 12, 1952.

*(James J. Buckley,
P. Allen Copeland Collection)*

The "three aces car", 111 was southbound on Warburton Ave. on July 11, 1952.

(James J. Buckley, P. Allen Copeland Collection)

The northern extension of Line 1 went north towards Hastings on Hudson, via Warburton Ave. After passing through downtown Yonkers at Getty Square, the cars went west a few blocks on Main Street and turned right onto Warburton Ave. This line was single tracked most of the way north with two passing sidings and offered passengers a scenic view of the Hudson River. The northern terminus was at the Yonkers City Limits. The line passed into history on in the wee hours of the morning of November 2, 1952.

Car 358 is southbound on Warburton Ave. waiting to turn left onto Main Street on October 25, 1952. In less than a week, the line will be abandoned and the car cut up for scrap.

(Lawson K. Hill, Boston Chapter, NRHS Collection)

Car 361 is Southbound on Park Ave. in a sparsely populated area of the northern reaches of Yonkers, September 1951. *(Eugene Van Dusen)*

1-2-3 Broadway in Yonkers

(Above) 144/350 passing on Ashburton siding on Warburton Ave. number 1 line. July 11, 1952. *(James J. Buckley, Allen P. Copeland Collection)*

(Below) In the northern part of the city of Yonkers, car 350 is southbound on Warburton Avenue, paralleling the Hudson River, on July 11, 1952. In July of that year the cars were still being kept fairly clean and cared for, but that policy would radically change by October when replacement bus deliveries began. *(James J. Buckley, Allen P. Copeland Collection)*

1-2-3 Broadway in Yonkers

4
MCLEAN AVENUE

Getty Square in Yonkers was the very last major street intersection in the New York City area available for photographing streetcars. Eight of the nine Yonkers lines passed through the complex trackwork at that point. Car 194 faces into the sun as it clatters across the specialwork enroute to the Bronx and its connection with the IRT Lexington-Jerome Avenues IRT subway/elevated line on July 12, 1952.
(J.J. Buckley, P. Allen Copeland Collection)

5
NEPPERHAN AVENUE

The 5- Nepperhan Avenue line originated at the foot of Main Street, Yonkers and operated on Main to Getty Square where it turned left into Palisade Avenue. It split from the 2 line at Elm and turned left from Elm onto Nepperhan where the line became a single track. After two passing sidings the line continued on the side of the road right-of-way to its northern terminal at Tompkins Avenue. It was abandoned on October 25, 1952.

Yonkers, like Rome was built on seven hills and this photo shows an inbound (i.e. southbound) car on Route 5-Nepperhan Avenue about to crest one of those hills. This point was where the side of the road right-of-way entered the center of the street for the ride to downtown Yonkers. It was roughly half way from Getty Square to the end of the line. When the line was originally built, the street was unpaved north of this point so the track was moved to the side of the road to allow paving to progress. The track area was never paved and one rail on the stretch was grooved girder rail while the other was Johnson rail reducing the possibility of derailments.
(Lawson K. Hill, Boston N.R.H.S. Collection)

McLean Avenue/Yonker Line 5 -Nepperhan Avenue

Car 341 lays over at the foot of Main Street, starting point for the 5 line with the New York Central Railroad station and Ferry terminal in background. July 22, 1951.
(James J. Buckley, P. Allen Copeland Collection)

Yonker Line 5 - Nepperhan Avenue

Car 346 is awaiting the light change at the corner of Main St. and Elm Street in Yonkers. The number 5 and 7 cars turned left here on their outbound runs. The track in the foreground was used by the inbound number 9- Elm Street cars. *(Bill Myers, Volkmer Collection)*

(Below) The operator of inbound car 394 appears to be having a conference with the operator of the outbound car, 372 during the waning days of car operation on the Nepperhan Ave. line. The scene is just north of the intersection with the 7 Yonkers Avenue line at the corner of Nepperhan and Yonkers Ave. in Yonkers. Not too far beyond camera range the line became single track on a narrow roadway and farther out, went to the side of the road in a very rural setting.
(Joel Diaz, P. Allen Copeland Collection)

(Left) Looking down Main Street at the Riverdale intersection with the foot of Main St. in the distance on May 20, 1951 we see cars 194 and 336 passing one another and riding into the setting sun. Indeed, a year and half later, car 194 would be the last car to ever operate in the Bronx. The author posseses the controller handle from this car to the present day. *(Eugene Van Dusen)*

Yonker Line 5 -Nepperhan Avenue

19

At the top of a hill, the single track veered off to the side where it stayed all the way to the Tompkins Ave. terminal. Enroute there were three passing sidings for meets with opposing cars. Here is car 381 inbound near the southern end of the private right of way.
(Lawson K. Hill, Boston Chapter, NRHS Collection)

Car 381 is just north of the Odell Avenue turnout on the same day, November 19, 1950.
(Lawson K. Hill, Boston Chapter, NRHS Collection)

The 193 was one of the 22 remaining 100-series cars in Yonkers at the end of service. The rest of the group had either been scrapped or sold when this photo was made, July 12, 1952 at the Tompkins Avenue terminal of the Nepperhan Ave. line.
(J.J. Buckley, P. Allen Copeland Collection)

Yonker Line 5 - Nepperhan Avenue

Car 106 looks forlorn during its last week of operation, seen on Main Street at Warburton Avenue in downtown Yonkers, October 25, 1952. *(Lawson K. Hill, Boston Chapter, NRHS Collection)*

7
YONKERS AVENUE

The 332 leaves the foot of Main Street in Yonkers on the morning of October 25, 1952 enroute to Mt. Vernon utilizing the number 7- Yonkers Avenue line. The battered and unwashed condition of the car portends the impending conclusion of once far-flung Third Avenue Railway System. *(Lawson K. Hill, Boston Chapter, NRHS Collection)*

Route 9 was the shortest and probably most obscure of the Yonkers streetcar lines. On July 12, 1952, car 387 holds down the lone assignment, resting between runs on the barn lead in front of the New York Central station. Passengers could transfer here for Chicago.
(J.J. Buckley, P. Allen Copeland Collection)

8
Riverdale Avenue

Yonkers line 8 Riverdale Avenue operated south from Main Street over Riverdale Avenue parallel to the Hudson River on single track to a point just north of the Bronx City Limits. It made its last run on October 25, 1952.

(Above) Car 340 changes ends at Riverdale and Main Street forcing those passengers destined for Getty Square to transfer to one of the many Main Street cars on October 25, 1952. *(Al Holtz)*

Rt. 7 Yonkers Ave

(Left) Route 7– Yonkers Avenue outlasted the other lines in Yonkers by one week and on November 8, 1952 saw the very last Third Avenue Railway streetcar run. In this scene, car 355 is eastbound on Yonkers Avenue in the late 1940s, headed towards the Mt. Vernon railroad station.

(Everett A. White, courtesy of Don Harold)

Third Avenue Railway in Manhattan

Over the years there were several Third Avenue Railway lines operating in the New Rochelle and Mt. Vernon areas of southern Westchester County, all inherited from the Westchester Electric Railway. In the post World War II era, these had been whittled down to just two lines that connected with the New York subway system. The A and B lines operated south from Mt. Vernon to the subway connection at White Plains Avenue and the Yonkers Number 7 line connected Mt. Vernon with Yonkers via Yonkers Avenue. This latter line came to hold the honor of being the very last Third Avenue line to operate. It was abandoned on November 8, 1952.

In the view taken at Mt. Vernon Station on November 19, 1950, one can compare the slightly differing roof lines between the 140 and the 300 series car in front of it. The 100s were constructed by stretching single truck cars. The old cars were first cut in half, four windows were added. Entirely new platforms were fabricated and attached to a much strengthened underframe. *(Lawson K. Hill, Boston Chapter, NRHS Collection)*

The 180 lays over at Mt. Vernon station, November 19, 1950. *(Lawson K. Hill, Boston Chapter, NRHS Collection)*

X
42ND ST. CROSSTOWN

There were seven streetcar lines operating in Manhattan during the World War II era. They were, the three "X" Crosstown lines, 42nd Street, the 59th Street, and the 125th St. Crosstown, plus the long, long (longest on the system!) T line, covering Third Avenue, 125th Street, and Amsterdam Avenue. A fifth route, "B", covered Broadway up to 129th and Amsterdam Ave. in Harlem. Two other routes, the K-Kingsbridge line operating in the far northern reaches of the island, and the 10th Avenue line rounded out rail surface transportation picture.

By June 28, 1947, a scant two years following the war's end, there were no car lines left in the borough. Buses and subways did it all.

59TH STREET CROSSTOWN

Less than three years old when the photo was taken May 30, 1942, car 638 was one of a group of 60 cars numbered 626 to 685 that were built in the company shops during 1938-39. The car is eastbound on the 59th Street Crosstown line at 5th Avenue, with Central Park in the background. This intersection is also known as Grand Army Plaza, not to be confused with the better-known one in Brooklyn. 59th Street at this point is better known as Central Park South, between 5th Avenue and 8th Avenue. It was and still is one of New York's best neighborhoods because of its view of Central Park.

(Lawson K. Hill, Boston Chapter, NRHS Collection)

(Above) The Hudson River ferry terminal on West 42nd Street in Manhattan was a good place to photograph the Third Ave. convertibles. The West Shore Ferry operation was very busy in its day. Here we see the 851 and 1058 with their sides removed in an attempt to keep the passengers cool during the steamy New York summers. The West Shore Ferry building can be seen behind the cars as can the Miller Highway. This West Side highway was ultimately torn down, before it had a chance to fall down. Historians will tell you that TARS 851 was the very first Brill convertible delivered to the railway. They are correct but this 851 is not that car. The original 851 was renumbered into the 600 series and after the new 600 series steel cars were built, it was renumbered 1142. Therefore, the car shown here is second number 851.

(Eugene Van Dusen)

(Left) The 554 is northbound on Broadway at Columbus Circle on May 30, 1942. It is interesting to note that this particular car was originally painted an experimental buff color and has already been returned to the standard Third Avenue Railway red and cream colors. Columbus Circle was one of the more photogenic spots in all of Manhattan for recording views of streetcars.

(Lawson K. Hill, Boston Chapter NRHS Collection)

IMPORTANT NOTICE

Effective Sunday, Nov. 10th 1946, buses will be operated in place of trolleys on the 59th Street Crosstown Line.

Your attention is called to changes in the route of the 59th Street line which will be operated as follows:

EASTBOUND: Along 59th Street between 10th Avenue and York Avenue.

WESTBOUND: Along 60th Street between York Avenue and Fifth Avenue and along 59th Street between Fifth Avenue and West End Avenue.

Transfers from North and South bound cars of the Third Avenue line to Westbound buses of the 59th Street line will be good at 60th Street and Third Avenue; and to Eastbound buses of the 59th Street line at 59th Street and Third Avenue as at present.

Third Avenue Railway in Manhattan

Third Avenue Railway in Manhattan

B
BROADWAY

Huffliner 597 (series 551-625, Company Shops 1936-38) is turning east onto 42nd Street from southbound 7th Avenue at Times Square on Memorial Day 1942. The car, one of 75, represented Third Avenue Railway's brief foray into the world of lightweight Peter Witt streetcar design, an idea which did not survive into the last large car construction project, the 600s which reverted to the front-entrance, rear exit concept.

(Lawson K. Hill, Boston Chapter, NRHS Collection)

Third Avenue Railway in Manhattan

The 601 is eastbound on 42nd Street between 6th and 5th Avenues, enroute to its terminal at 1st Avenue and 42nd Street.
(Bill Volkmer Collection)

X- 42ND STREET CROSSTOWN

(Left) Convertible car 1075 operates a November 1946 fantrip on Broadway, above 59th Street. The 42nd St. "Crosstown" sign on the side of the deck roof is where some ambitious railfan has scraped the gray paint off the glass. The roofs' original "salmon" color were painted gray with the advent of World War II blackouts. At that time they simply painted over the glass "Crosstown" signs. *(Eugene Van Dusen)*

(Left) The 42nd Street Crosstown line operated straight as an arrow from the East River in an area called Tudor City, past Times Square, to the ferry terminal at 12th Avenue and the Hudson River. Portions of the route were shared with the B-Broadway as well as the ferry terminal being shared with the 10th Avenue line. During the weekdays convertible cars plied the route, but on Sundays and holidays the newer 600 series cars took over. On May 30, 1942, a holiday, car 643, then only four years young operated eastbound on 42nd Street at 7th Avenue, Times Square. The 643 was later sold to Bombay, India, but not until it served a brief time in the Bronx operating with trolley poles along the 167th Street Crosstown line.
(Lawson K. Hill, Boston Chapter, NRHS Collection)

(Left) Convertible car 1101 is at the eastern end of the 42nd Street Crosstown line near the East River on October 19, 1946.
(Lawson K. Hill, Boston Chapter, NRHS Collection)

OFF TO BRAZIL

(Above) Three Peter Witt-design Third Ave. cars (known locally as the Huffliners) are shown here loaded on a barge for later transloading to a ship bound for Sao Paulo, Brazil. The locale is the Erie Basin district in Brooklyn. Once in Brazil, the cars would have a trolley pole added and be converted to single end operation. There they would operate for an additional 20 years. Two specimens were preserved in Brazil, one in a park and a second in a Sao Paulo museum, where they ostensibly remain to this date. *(Everett A. White, courtesy of Don Harold)*

T- Third Avenue

The end of the 163rd St. Crosstown line was actually across the river in Manhattan at 155th Street and Amsterdam. Here car 118 has passed by a Fifth Avenue Motor Coach double decker bus seen in the distance as is the Polo Grounds, then home to the New York Giants baseball team. "Then" was March 13, 1948. Now the Giants play in San Francisco and only buses ply 161st St. Whereas many of the other 100 series cars went on to serve in Yonkers, Bombay, India, and Lima, Peru, following the demise of this line on June 25, 1948, this car was apparently scrapped. *(Lawson Hill, Boston Chapter, NRHS Collection)*

One-of a kind car 1259 is at 155th St. near Amsterdam in Manhattan. When it was originally built in 1934, it was numbered 1605. The photo was taken March 13, 1948 a year and a half before the line was abandoned but only two months before the car itself was sent to scrap.
(Lawson Hill, Boston Chapter, NRHS Collection)

OVERHEAD WIRE IN MANHATTAN

The only places that overhead wire was allowed to be strung over streetcar trackage in the borough of Manhattan were the few spots where Bronx lines briefly crossed over the Harlem River and entered the borough to terminate, where passengers could transfer to a Manhattan bound car. One such place is illustrated on this page, the western end of the 163rd Street Crosstown line the Bronx. Passengers could board from a conduit-powered car operating along upper Broadway and go to Yankee Stadium or the Polo Grounds.

T- Amsterdam Avenue

Southbound car 180 is on Amsterdam Ave., probably near 181st Street in the mid-1940s. Amsterdam Ave was notable for its extraordinarily wide devil strip between the tracks owing to its unusual width. This was the suburbs when the line was constructed. *(Anscochrome slide, Lawson K. Hill, Boston Chapter, NRHS Collection)*

TARS 138 is passing City Hall on Park Row in lower Manhattan in April 1947. At this point the car lacks about one block of finishing its long run on the Third Avenue-Amsterdam Ave. line. *(Everett A. White, courtesy Don Harold)*

On April 14, 1946 a railfan charter by the Electric Railroaders' Association toured several of the Bronx and Manhattan lines using car 990, a curved side convertible, out of the Kingsbridge carhouse. Karl Groh was aboard and vividly recalls the events of the day. Many of the fans were newly returned from the service and were eager to film the remaining conduit operated lines before their impending demise in favor of diesel buses that had recently come into vogue with the advent of the automatic transmissions.

The 990 is southbound on Bailey Ave. paralleling the New York Central Railroad tracks. The car was one of a 200-car order built by Brill in 1909, and had recently received a new coat of paint. The paint would last another two years as the car was finally scrapped in May 1948 following cessation of the remaining Manhattan trolley lines in June of 1947 and many of the Bronx routes as well.
(Lawson Hill, Boston Chapter, NRHS Collection)

(Left) The trip later operated over the 138th Street Crosstown line to its eastern terminus at E. 138th and Locust Avenue. A photo opportunity prevailed while the operator changed ends on the 990 for the return trip westward.
(Lawson Hill, Boston Chapter, NRHS Collection)

(Right) While the fans were photographing the 990, a regular car, number 5, one of the remaining straight side convertibles pulled onto 138th Street from Locust Avenue off a short single track spur that operated down to E. 134th Street, along the East River. April 14, 1946.
(Lawson Hill, Boston Chapter, NRHS Collection)

(Below) Special car 990 has now changed ends at 138th St. and the East River and is about to depart westward.
(Lawson Hill, Boston Chapter, NRHS Collection)

(Below) This scene shows the southernmost point reached by the Third Avenue Railway, opposite the City Hall in Manhattan. This was once the site of New York's main Post Office, but it was torn down to make way for City Hall Park. The cars continued to carry the Post Office destination long after the building had been razed. To the left of the photographer was the terminal structure for the 3rd Avenue elevated. It too was torn down a few years after the streetcars were taken out. *(Lawson Hill, Boston Chapter, NRHS Collection)*

Bronx and Manhattan Railfan Tour

August 21, 1948 spelled the end for streetcar operation in the Bronx Borough of New York City. On that date, other than the short stretches of rail operating into the Bronx from Yonkers, only buses provided surface transportation. All that remained at that time were five trolley lines, out of the dozens that once permeated the cityscape there. Over the next few pages, we shall see a sampling of a New York that once was; a city where people were friendlier and the pace a bit less hectic than in later years. The demise of the streetcar in the Bronx began just prior to World War II at a time when the heaviest rail lines were extensively modernized using new cars built in the company shops and used cars purchased from a variety of other U.S. cities. By 1946, heavy wartime usage of the trolleys had taken its toll on the mechanical integrity of the cars, and the political climate of the day dictated a conversion to buses rather than the purchase of PCC cars. At first, there was a plan to keep five Bronx lines until 1960 in order to amortize 20 years out of the newest cars. However, a five-year plan was soon put into place to convert all of the remaining Third Avenue Railway streetcars by 1951. Conversion began in 1946/47 in Manhattan, then spread like a cancer to the Bronx in 47/48, and finally in 1950 to the Westchester County lines and Yonkers in November 1952.

One of Third Avenue's newest cars, 666, is running its last miles in the Bronx on August 21, 1948. No Bronx streetcar lines remained after that date except for the two or three that touched into the north Bronx from Yonkers, those lasting for another four years. Railfans had lifted all of the dash signs by this time so a hand lettered "T" was painted on the dasher. The last lines to operate in this area were the T- Tremont St., S- Southern Boulevard, V- Williamsburg Bridge, and B- Boston Road. The summers in the Bronx were very hot, and air conditioned streetcars and subways were non-existent. Car 666, because of its young age, was sold to Vienna where it operated as car 4214 for several more years before final retirement and scrapping.
(Eugene Van Dusen)

We present this photo to illustrate how the Third Avenue convertible cars appeared during the hot, sticky summer months in New York City. The sides were removed in early May, stored in the car house, and reinstalled at the end of September. Car 285 operates westbound on the Z-180th Street Crosstown line at Bathgate Avenue with the Third Avenue elevated structure in the background. *(Karl Groh)*

The Westchester Avenue line operated up and down Westchester Avenue in the Bronx, between Tremont Avenue on the north, and the intersection of Westchester and 3rd Avenues (known as "The Hub") on the south. The majority of the route operated in the shadow of the elevated structure overhead, making it difficult to photograph. The late afternoon sun helped when this photo was made of car 675 on March 13, 1948 at the intersection of 163rd Street and Westchester Avenue. At that point, passengers could transfer to the 163rd Street Crosstown line in addition to a ride on the elevated downtown. All this came to an end on July 11, 1948 when the line was abandoned. The 163rd St. line was abandoned two weeks prior. *(Lawson K. Hill, Boston Chapter NRHS Collection)*

A WESTCHESTER AVENUE

L- ST. ANNS AVENUE

(Right) The L line, St. Anns Avenue, only ran between 161st and 134th Streets in later years. It originally ran over 133rd Street to the el station of the 2nd and 3rd Ave elevateds. It was truncated when the S- Southern Boulevard line was abandoned on 133rd Street, a line with which it shared 133rd Street. The route designation "L" came from the fact that on the map, the line formed the letter "L". Rush hour cars ran on 138th Street to 8th Avenue in Manhattan, but this operation was discontinued prior to World War II. Car 829, pictured here on October 19, 1946, ran most of its life on the 59th St. Crosstown line in Manhattan until 1939 when it was "bumped" by the newer 626-645 class cars. After 1939 it had poles fitted, as shown here, along with sister cars 821, 823, 828, 829 and 830 for service on St. Anns Avenue. The St. Anns line was abandoned, along with the 167th Street Crosstown line, on July 10, 1948.
(Lawson K. Hill, Boston Chapter, NRHS Collection)

(Left) There were five semi-convertible cars saved from the 59th Street Crosstown line in 1938 when that line received more modern cars. Cars 821, 823, 828-830 were equipped with trolley poles, shipped to West Farms Carhouse on 175th Street at Boston Road, and were used on the St. Anns Avenue line as well as the 138th Street Crosstown line. Only three cars were needed for the L line. Many of the sister cars in this group were sold to Quebec City and San Diego. Car 830 of the group was saved and sent to the Shoreline Trolley Museum in Branford, Connecticut. Sale price for the museum cars in 1948 was $1.00. Car 823 is shown on April 14, 1946 outside the West Farms carhouse on the street between the old building (shown in the background) and the new building (where the track in the foreground leads). The old original barn was recently town down and the new building was used into the 1990s by the IRT signal department.
(Lawson K. Hill, Boston Chapter, NRHS Collection)

149th Street Crosstown

(Left) This photo is not the best, but is included here for two reasons. First, it shows Third Avenue cars operating in the open configuration and second, because it depicts Karl Groh's boyhood home. Karl grew up looking out the window behind the A&P sign in the photo. If that wouldn't make a trolley fan out of a young boy, what would? The view shows car 75 crossing over just west of St. Anns Avenue on the 149th Street crosstown line. Three blocks west, behind the dewired car, lies the junction of 149th Street, Third Avenue, Melrose, Westchester and Willis Avenue, known as "The Hub", in the Bronx.
(Karl Groh Collection)

163rd STREET CROSSTOWN LINE

The 163rd Street line operated across the heart of the Bronx, serving the Polo Grounds at 155th St. and 8th Avenue, former home of the National League New York Giants, Yankee Stadium at 161st Street and River Avenue, over Elton Avenue and 163rd Street joining Hunts Point Road at Southern Boulevard. The eastern terminal was at Randall Avenue and Hunts Point.

(Below) Dingy looking, but soldiering on to the bitter end was this former San Antonio, Texas warrior, number 1244. It is operating on the 163rd Street Crosstown line, westbound just a block or two east of Third Avenue in the Bronx. In San Antonio, these cars operated on rare 4'0" gauge track, so when that system was motorized, the bodies were loaded aboard a ship and brought to New York. New Brill 77E trucks were used under the cars until the new 100 series carbuilding program, begun in 1934, needed them. At that time, second-hand C-55 trucks were placed under these 1200s running on University Ave. until the 1230-1248 were reassigned to the 163rd Street run. *(Lawson K. Hill, Boston Chapter, NRHS Collection)*

V- Williamsbridge

The Williamsbridge line was named after a locality, rather than a street as was the common practice in the Bronx. It began at Gun Hill Road and White Plains Ave. and went south on White Plains until it reached Morris Park Ave. where it turned into Morris Park and shared trackage with the B- Boston Road as far as West Farms Square. Some cars turned back at West Farms but most continued on Tremont Avenue to 3rd Ave which was the western terminal using a rare-for-the-Bronx facing point crossover. Car 141 is approaching that crossover in this undated photo. Out of the picture behind the camera is the Tremont Ave. – 177th Street station of the 3rd Ave. elevated. *(Everett A. White, courtesy of Don Harold)*

(Below) Car 124 is westbound at West Farms Square. This extremely busy trolley enclave was one of the places that first introduced the author to the world of trolleys (at age 10) as he gazed out the window of an elevated train while being taken to the Bronx Zoo on Labor Day, 1946.
(Everett A. White, courtesy of Don Harold)

S- Southern Boulevard

Southern Boulevard received brand new 600 series cars in 1939. Cars 646-685 had poles installed for both the S and T lines when built. An additional fifteen cars were planned, but never constructed, because of Mayor LaGuardia's anti-streetcar stance. Here, car 652 is seen operating on Southern Blvd. at E. 175th Street, the last day of streetcar operation, August 21, 1948. The car was a scant nine years old.
(Eugene Van Dusen)

The Southern Boulevard line was a long north-south trunk line that connected 189th Street near Bronx Park with 138th Street on the south. It was one of the last lines to be motorized in the Bronx, on August 21, 1948.

The southern terminus of the S- Southern Boulevard line was one of the more interesting spots on the Third Avenue system. The line terminated at 138th and Bruckner Blvd., which was formerly Eastern Blvd. After the southbound (i.e. inbound) car changed ends and proceeded through the facing point switch where a traffic light pre-empter stopped northbound auto traffic, allowing the streetcar to enter back onto Bruckner. About four blocks north, Southern Boulevard branched off of Bruckner to the left. In this photo, 654 is waiting for the light to change, while 176 has just arrived and the operator is taking a break before pulling south, past the switch to change ends.
(Everett W. White, courtesy of Don Harold)

W- WEBSTER AVENUE
WHITE PLAINS AVENUE

The W- Webster-White Plains Ave. line was one of the main north-south trunk lines paralleling the subway-elevated routes that permeated the Bronx. It ran due north and south from 242nd Street on the north, down White Plains Avenue to Gun Hill, over Gun Hill to south on Webster. At 163rd St. the name Webster changed into Melrose and the cars terminated just north of 149th St. on Melrose. Prior to 1941, one could transfer and continue south by streetcar down Willis Avenue to 125th Street and across Manhattan to the Edgewater Ferry at 12th Avenue and 125th Street. Last run on the Webster-White Plains was on June 26, 1948. The second hand cars from Staten Island and other sources were the mainstays of this line.

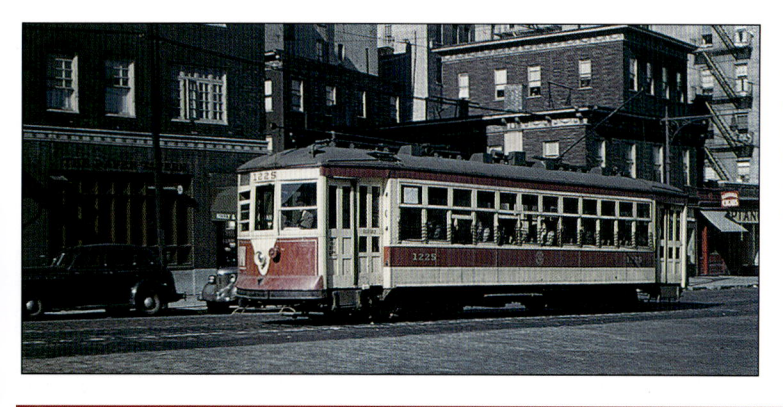

Second hand car 1225 originally ran on Richmond Railways (numbered 425 there) in Staten Island. It is shown southbound on the W- Webster Avenue line, north of Fordham Road, on October 19, 1946. New track and new cobblestones had been installed at this location in 1939. The Harlem Division of the New York Central R.R. is in a cut behind the photographer.
(Anscochrome slide, Lawson K. Hill, Boston Chapter, NRHS Collection)

Z- 180TH STREET CROSSTOWN

So as to not confuse patrons using the 167th Street Crosstown line which shared a portion of the route, the 180th Street line was known as the "Z" line. It ran from 181st St. and Broadway in Manhattan's upper west side eastward over Tremont Ave. and 180th Street, past West Farms Square, and over 177th Street to Unionport, terminating at Bruckner Boulevard.

Westbound Z line car 294 is atop the Washington Bridge spanning the Harlem River (not to be confused with the nearby George Washington suspension bridge) and the six-track main line of the New York Central on the Bronx shore line. This bridge served four car lines and connected three Bronx thoroughfares with 181st Street in Manhattan. Car lines O, X, U and Z terminated just west of this site at Broadway, (without track connection of course) in Manhattan's Washington Heights section. It was one of only four streets in Manhattan borough having overhead wire. Others were 135th St., 155th Street, and 207th Street. The red brick apartment houses at the left are on Amsterdam Avenue, the only place in all of New York where overhead wire crossed a conduit operated (Amsterdam Ave.) line. The Unionport destination on the rear of the car indicates the other terminal for the Z line. The photo was taken October 19, 1946 and the line was abandoned on August 21, 1948, one of the last four car lines to operated in the Bronx proper.
(Anscochrome slide, Lawson K. Hill, Boston Chapter, NRHS Collection)

T- Tremont Avenue

The last of the series 301-400, car 400 ran most of its life on the T- Tremont Avenue line out of West Farms barn, but towards the end it is seen here on Route B- Boston Road. It is shown at the south terminal at 138th Street and 3rd Avenue on March 13, 1948. The "B" destination plate covers the "T" painted on the dash. Car 32 usually ran on 167th Street Crosstown, but was bumped to the "extra list" when 600 series cars from Manhattan arrived with newly fitted trolley poles and took over 167th Street Crosstown route duties. 100 series cars (101-200) also ran on Boston Road and many other Bronx lines with trolley poles affixed. At the extreme right hand side of the photo, one can almost see the Inspector with his day sheet.

(Lawson K. Hill, Boston Chapter, NRHS Collection)

The intersection of Valentine, Tremont, and Webster avenues made for some very interesting streetcar watching in the 1940s, probably a close second to neighboring West Farms Square. 673 is heading towards West Farms in the mid-1940s. The T- Tremont along with S- Southern Boulevard were the two routes that inherited the Manhattan 600 series cars following the demise of the conduit lines there.

(Everett A. White, courtesy of Don Harold)

Car 380 is seen passing the Crotona theater on Tremont Ave. between 3rd Avenue and Webster avenue. This particular stretch of the Tremont Avenue line was very slow running due to the terrible traffic congestion, even in the 1940s when the picture was taken. *(Everett A. White, courtesy of Don Harold)*

This scene is looking east on Tremont Avenue from the 3rd Avenue El station as car 181 traverses one of the three facing point single crossovers in the Bronx. The crossover was used for the V-Williamsbridge cars to turn back at this point. The V line overlapped the T line through West Farms Square to Morris Park Avenue, at which point it turned northward.
(Everett A. White, courtesy of Don Harold)

It appears to be an unusually quiet day in the Bronx, with only a single lone automobile in sight as the 380 passes by the Bronx Savings Bank. This scene looks northwest on Tremont Street at Westchester Avenue.
(Everett A. White, courtesy of Don Harold)

39

(Left) Originally built for Manhattan without poles, car 643 now sports trolley poles for operation on Route A- Westchester Avenue in the Bronx. Here is southbound at E 163rd Street and Westchester Avenue. The Route X 163rd Street car is a high roof 100 series, westbound and it also ran in Manhattan most of its life before getting trolley poles. The elevated structure in the background carries the IRT subway trains of the Lexington and 7th Avenue lines, now known as Route 2, to 241st St. and the Route 5 Dyre Avenue line. The structure here carries the tracks straight over a valley with the Intervale Avenue station in the middle, one of the highest stations on the IRT. Only 125th & Broadway is higher.
(Lawson K. Hill, Boston Chapter, NRHS Collection)

(Left) Car 38 represents a group of 100 straight sided convertible cars built by J.G. Brill in 1908. Between the straight and curved sided convertibles, Third Avenue operated a fleet of over 400. This was the Third Avenue's signature car model until the mid-1930s when the fleet was extensively modernized. The 1-100 series cars were originally built as conduit cars but all were eventually equipped with poles for dual, conduit/overhead operation. Many of the convertible cars were scrapped in order to salvage seats, hardware, bells etc. for new cars being built in the 1930s. TARS was a very frugal operation to say the least. *(Frank Watson)*

(Right) Car 276 is one of 100 straight side convertible cars built by J.G. Brill in 1908 as a Pay-As-You-Enter type car. This was the only group of convertibles built with poles and none ever operated on conduit lines. It is shown operating in its closed (i.e. winter) configuration at West Farms Square on the Z- 180th Street Crosstown line. The car did not survive the end of Bronx streetcar service in August 1948, as it was scrapped in Mt. Vernon, the previous May.
(Frank Watson)

THIRD AVENUE RAILWAY COMPANY ROSTER SHOTS

(Right) In 1934-35 Third Avenue Railway shops turned out 100 lightweight steel cars on Brill 77E trucks, rebuilt from old 39E trucks. Many of the parts came from the 49 surviving old single-truck convertibles numbered 101-150 which probably accounts for the choice of number sequence. These cars were originally assigned to the Manhattan conduit lines, but had trolley poles added at a later date. Car 111, shown here in Yonkers on July 11, 1952, was built in December 1935 and remained in service until the end, being scrapped November 17, 1952. Twenty of this series cars were sold to Lima, Peru in 1947 and twenty-five of this series were sold to Bombay, India in 1949. Twenty-three of the remaining 55 cars survived until the end of service while the rest were cannibalized and scrapped for parts during the last few years of system operation. *(J.J. Buckley, P. Allen Copeland Collection)*

(Right) Car 321, shown at the Garden Avenue Yard in Mt. Vernon, was one of a group of 100 cars built in the Company Shops on 3rd Avenue at 65th Street in 1935-37. The cars were very similar in design to the 100 series built in the two previous years and also similar to the 600 series cars built in 1938. Unlike the 100 series, several of this series were equipped with trolley poles at the time of construction. 58 of the 100 cars were in service at the end, in November 1952. *(Frank Watson)*

(Left) The original prototype Huffliner (75 cars), car 551 is shown here at the lead to the Kingsbridge Carhouse in upper Manhattan. The carhouse was located at 218th Street and 10th Avenue, at the point where Broadway and 10th Avenue merged. At the time this photo was made, in November 1946, the B- Broadway line had already been converted to buses, so the car ran its last miles on the K- Kingsbridge line. After streetcar service in Manhattan was discontinued, all 75 cars were sold to Sao Paulo Brazil, where two cars have reportedly been preserved. *(Eugene Van Dusen)*

(Left) Behind Kingsbridge carhouse, where the 1210 was photographed in November 1946, there was a barge landing on the Harlem River. It was at this location that the Railway received bulk commodities such as sand and rail to be distributed about the far-flung system. The 1210, a former Staten Island car had been in an accident and had the opposite end from the one in the photograph extensively rebuilt. It was at this location that all 75 Huffliners were loaded aboard barges for the short trip to Erie Basin on the Brooklyn waterfront. A photo of this appeared earlier on page 29. Once in Brooklyn, they were loaded on seagoing freighters and transported to Brazil. The Harlem River was too shallow for oceangoing ships. *(Eugene Van Dusen)*

(Right) The 665 represents arguably one of the very last non-PCC streetcars ever built in America. It was turned out of the TARS' 65th Street shops in 1939 as a part of a group of 38 cars numbered 646-685. These cars were originally equipped with trolley poles for operation in the Bronx. They immediately followed a similar group of 20 conduit operated cars numbered 626-645. The conduit cars were used to modernize the 59th Street Crosstown line and saw weekend service on the 42nd Street line as well. 40 of the 58 cars were sold to Vienna, Austria in 1949 where they were equipped with pantographs. 15 others were sold to Bombay, India. The 665, pictured here at 138th Street and 3rd Avenue on March 13, 1948, became Vienna 4203.
(Lawson K. Hill, Boston Chapter, NRHS Collection)

Garden Avenue Yard

(Right) An overall view of the yard shows a variety of single truck cars from which the Branford preservationists and a plethora of souvenir hunters took their pick.
(Everett A. White, courtesy of Don Harold)

(Above) Sand car 19 was one of eight single truck 16 foot cars that were converted to sand car service for the Union Railway in 1913. It was scrapped at this site in March 1948.
(Everett A. White, courtesy of Don Harold)

Garden Avenue Yard in Mount Vernon was the place where the railway sent all of their surplus cars for cannibalization and eventual scrapping. In the period around 1947-48, it was a veritable cornucopia for railfans seeking to collect artifacts from cars withdrawn from service. Pictured on this page are scenes from that latter day era, probably the summer of 1947.

(Left) Car 327 has apparently been set aside as a source of parts to keep the remainder of the fleet operable. Many of the other 300s would last another five years performing service in Yonkers.
(Everett A. White, courtesy of Don Harold)

(Left) Car 1085 was obviously a casualty of the 10th Avenue abandonment which went bus on November 18, 1946.

(Everett A. White, courtesy of Don Harold)

2

Brooklyn & Queens Transit

The borough of Brooklyn during the 1940s and early 1950s was criss-crossed by about 40 streetcar lines operating out of no less than seven carhouses, or "depots" as they were known in Brooklyn. A few of the northernmost lines ventured into Queens as well. Indeed, there were so many trolleys operating in Brooklyn that the local National League baseball team derived its name from the cars, being called the Brooklyn Trolley Dodgers, shortened of course, to just the "Dodgers."

During the 1920s and '30s the mainstay of the Brooklyn and Queens Transit was its fleet of deck-roof convertible cars, built shortly after the turn of the century. In the mid-1920s, with the swing towards one-man operation, a large fleet of Peter Witt cars, 525 over two years, was purchased. In 1930 this concept was broadened with purchase of an additional 200 Peter Witts, and in 1936, Brooklyn became the first city in America to endorse the concept of the PCC car, by purchasing 100.

Beginning in the mid-1930s, Fiorello LaGuardia, the sometimes controversial mayor of New York, lead the charge to rid the streets of New York City of streetcar rails. One of his cronies, city planning commissioner, Robert Moses was busy designing arterial highways which further decimated the streetcar infrastructure. Accordingly, the number of car lines was reduced until World War II, with its rubber and fuel shortages put a moratorium on streetcar abandonments. Following the end of the war, abandonment of rail lines and bus substitution accelerated, with many lines being converted to trolley coach operation in order to take advantage of the existing power facilities. By 1951, the Brooklyn system had been reduced to but three main trunk lines, all served by PCCs exclusively. They were the McDonald Avenue, Coney Island Avenue and Church Avenue lines. Almost all non-PCC cars had gone to scrap by the time that railfan color photography came into common use.

When the 100 car PCC fleet became fully amortized in 1956, those last three lines were also abandoned, ending the streetcar era in New York City, with the lone exception of the Queensborough Bridge line, which lasted into 1957. Electric trolley bus operation was discontinued in Brooklyn on July 26, 1960.

■ ■ ■

During the World War II era in Brooklyn there was a huge variety of streetcars operating, in addition to the 100 PCC cars. There were a small group of center entrance cars on the Norton's Point line, Peter Witt cars of two distinct varieties, and a group of ancient deck roof cars, some convertible and some semi-convertible. The borough was truly a trolley fan's paradise, the giant subway/elevated system, above and below, notwithstanding. On these pages, we shall sample what Brooklyn had to offer in those halcyon days gone by.

In 1930 Brooklyn had about 300 miles of streetcar track and about 1800 cars. Of the 1800, 525 were fairly new, five to six-year old Peter Witts (8000 series). 200 more modern Peter Witts all single-end design were delivered in 1930-31 and 100 PCC cars came in 1936. Thus during the final twelve years of operation that are covered in this book, there were about 825 modern cars plus a few dozen "relics" to be photographed.

Car 8310, a double ended Peter Witt car is operating eastbound along some single track running on Meserole St. at Lorimer in 1949. The Lorimer St. tracks in the foreground were not connected to Meserole and were later converted to the 48- Lorimer electric bus line. *(Everett A. White, courtesy of Don Harold)*

44

WILSON AVENUE LINE

The Wilson Avenue line (renamed from Hamburg Avenue a German city, in 1917, to favor then President Woodrow Wilson) was originally a seven-plus mile long line operating from the Williamsburg Bridge Plaza over Broadway, Meserole and Johnson Avenues to Morgan Avenue down to Wilson, then over Cooper which changed its name to Rockaway Ave. at Broadway and changed names again at Foster Avenue to Rockaway Parkway, all the way to Canarsie Shore. In the early 1930s, the B&QT was building loops around town in anticipation of operating the single-ended 6000 series Peter Witt cars, but they found that Wilson Ave. was too narrow to accept these cars. Hence the 4100 series convertibles held down the run until 8000 series Peter Witts were made available for service on the route at the tail end of rail operation.

The subway-elevated line to Canarsie Shore, which duplicated the Rockaway Parkway portion of the Wilson Ave. streetcar line, was cut back to the Rockaway Parkway surface crossing around 1928 when new subway equipment was purchased without trolley poles. As a replacement for the subway/el cars, eight deck-roof 4700 series cars (rebuilt from older 3700 and 3900 series stock) were then operated over the former elevated line (at grade) tracks, as a shuttle streetcar operation, from the end of the subway to a new loop that had been constructed at Canarsie Shore. Both the streetcar line and the elevated line had formerly been stub-ended at that location.

In 1939 the Wilson Avenue line was cut back to a point north of the Belt Parkway construction site, because of a combination of the construction of the new Belt Parkway through the heart of Canarsie Shore, and a general decline in patronage at the old Golden City park. In 1944, the Wilson cars were terminated at Canarsie Depot because of wartime car shortages and a shuttle was operated from there to the Canarsie-Rockaway subway/el station where a connection was made with the Canarsie Shuttle. The Wilson shuttle operated the short stretch northward between the subway station and Hegeman Ave. until May 27, 1951, at which time the Wilson shuttle was absorbed into bus line B60-Wilson Avenue, and the Canarsie Shuttle over Rockaway Parkway was converted to a bus route also.

(Above) B&QT 761 was truly a soldier doing wartime duty on October 18, 1943. She is in the process of changing ends at 39th Street and New Utrecht Avenue. The car was built in 1898 by the American Car Company with open-end platforms, standard fare at that time. It was rebuilt with closed ends about 1906 and then extensively rebuilt in 1920 as a pay-as-you-enter car. *(Lawson K. Hill, Boston Chapter, NRHS)*

(Above) Car 2568 is shown here on the West End surface line October 18, 1943 leaving the private right of way formerly used by elevated trains (originally the Brooklyn, Bath and West End Railroad). The elevated structure was built over New Utrecht Avenue and 86th Street, and right-of-way was turned over to streetcars serving Bath Avenue. It was repaved when the el trains went upstairs. Note "West End" on the roll sign and the elevated structure in the distance. Surface cars ran between 39th Street/ New Utrecht Ave. and Harway Avenue loop all year. From June to September the line was extended to Coney Island. 8200 series Peter Witt cars served the line during the summer and these old deck roofed cars the rest of the year. These consisted of cars in the 700 and 1100 series, including the 797 and 798 that were originally parlor cars.

(Lawson K. Hill, Boston Chapter, NRHS)

45

Wilson Avenue Shuttle

The Wilson Avenue car line, prior to 1930, ran all the way from the Williamsburg section of Brooklyn to Canarsie Shore utilizing two fare zones. Around 1930, the second zone, the area between Canarsie Depot and Canarsie Shore, operating along Rockaway Parkway, was split away and renamed the Rockaway Parkway line. In 1937 the two lines were re-combined, but a year later, in 1938 the two lines were again separated. Because of the ongoing construction of the Belt Parkway near Canarsie Shore and the demolition of Golden City Park, the line was cut back in 1939 to a switch on Rockaway Parkway at Skidmore Avenue. Following the rerouting of the Canarsie Shuttle onto Rockaway Parkway on November 21, 1942, the Wilson Avenue line was extended to Rockaway Parkway station and shared the terminal loop with the new Rockaway Parkway Line. Because of wartime car shortages, in the summer of 1944 it became necessary to cut the Wilson Ave. line back to Canarsie Depot and substitute a shuttle line the remainder of the way to Rockaway Parkway, requiring only two cars. In 1944 the two cars were 2500 series convertibles, but following the war 8000 series cars had become surplus and were used on the line. In the photo above, we see car 8190 heading north towards Carnarsie Depot (Hegeman Ave.) just north of the Long Island Rail Road - Bay Ridge branch overpass on Rockaway Avenue. The shuttle was abandoned on May 27, 1951. *(Everett A. White, courtesy of Don Harold)*

This photo of Peter Witt 8408 is a puzzler. The sign, St. Johns is definitely wrong as this street is too narrow to be St. Johns Place, which was a wide street. The car is a low 8400, so it was working out of Canarsie Depot and MAY be on the Wilson Ave. line, a narrow street. Center route sign seems to say WILSON and side front sign not readable, but single-end routes like Wilson, that had double-end cars on them frequently had "wrong" signs on the other end, as operators seldom ventured to the back of the car to change signs unless the inspector ordered them to do so. The St. John's line had low 8100 series high-speed cars assigned to it. Our only other guess is it's on Putnam Ave. but high 8400s out of Fresh Pond Depot operated there. One other possibility would be Cooper Ave. also a narrow street. Single end 6000s were tried out on Wilson, but the street was too narrow with too many scrapes with automobiles, causing a return to the older double-ended cars.
(Photo from Eugene Van Dusen remarks by Karl F. Groh

Brooklyn's Conventional Streetcars

Canarsie Shore Shuttle

The Canarsie Shore loop was built in the early 1920s for use by the streetcars that replaced elevated trains formerly operated to that point. The elevated platforms, with one exception, were torn down when the streetcars took over, but some elevated trains, equipped with trolley poles, continued to be used for special events at Golden City Park such as fireworks shows etc. When the 14th Street subway line was extended to Rockaway Parkway in 1928, eight B&QT convertible cars of the 3700 and 3900 series were rebuilt into single-end closed cars, renumbered 4700-4707, and were operated as a shuttle and as a part of the rapid transit system. On November 21, 1942, the line was rerouted from its private-right-of-way onto the parallel Rockaway Parkway, utilizing the tracks of that line, but terminating at the subway terminal on a loop jointly shared with the Wilson Ave. shuttle cars. The right of way was abandoned and the rails torn up as scrap for the war effort. This photo of car 4705 was taken on the loop on July 25, 1945. In the final analysis, these eight cars represented the last operation of deck roof streetcars in revenue service in Brooklyn, being taken off on April 26, 1948. 8000 series Peter Witt cars served the line until its abandonment on May 27, 1951. No fare was charged to ride on this line if the passenger had come from the subway. Fares were collected only outside the terminal area of the Rockaway Parkway station, as the trolley line was considered to be a part of the rapid transit line. No paper transfers were used.

(Lawson K. Hill, Boston Chapter, NRHS Collection, Information from Don Harold and Karl Groh)

Last Days At Canarsie Depot

The photo below shows Canarsie Depot yard in May 1951. There are no red Peter Witt cars, no 6000 series Peter Witts, nor are there any PCC cars in sight. At this time, the last few car lines operating out of this depot, Ocean Avenue, Ralph-Rockaway, the Canarsie Shuttle, Wilson Shuttle etc. were fast going out of existence. Since February 11, 1951 PCCs had served the Church Avenue line that looped near the Depot owing to a mandate by the Brooklyn Trust Co., owners of the PCC cars must be stored indoors. This necessitated their being based at the indoor Ninth Avenue Depot. The last red streetcar to operate in Brooklyn had done so on April 30, 1951, but there was one red car stored out of sight in the building at Canarsie. That car was the 8111 which was being saved for preservation at Branford Museum. Following the abandonment of the Ralph-Rockaway and the Canarsie Shuttle on May 27, 1951, all but 20 of these veterans made a final run to the Avenue X Yard, site of one giant bonfire. *(Eugene Van Dusen)*

Brooklyn's Conventional Streetcars

FLATBUSH AVENUE LINE

The Flatbush Avenue line was probably Brooklyn's heaviest patronized surface line because it served the main part of the downtown business district. 6000-6199 series Peter Witts, built in 1930 and '31, immediately preceding the PCC era, held down the route in later years. It is said that the reason PCCs were not utilized on the line was because they could not be stored indoors during inclement weather. The Flatbush cars always operated from the Flatbush Depot at Avenue N and Utica Ave. The line operated from the Tillary Street loop near the Borough Hall and Brooklyn Bridge southward along Livingston and Flatbush to the loop at Flatbush and Avenue U. The line was converted to buses in 1951 essentially ending the tenure of the modern Peter Witt cars in Brooklyn.

A September 10, 1949 view of Tillary St. loop in downtown Brooklyn shows Peter Witt car 6048 laying over between runs on the Flatbush Avenue line. This long line sliced through the very heart of Brooklyn tapping many parks and recreation venues such as Ebbetts Field, home of the Brooklyn Dodgers. This line had two south terminals, one at Avenue U and Flatbush, the other being at E. 71st Street and Avenue N. Note the Brooklyn tower of the Manhattan Bridge showing in the background of the photo. The Sands Street elevated structure that once stood near this spot was torn down in 1943 and converted into battleships etc. for the war effort. *(Eugene Van Dusen)*

METROPOLITAN AVENUE LINE

The nine-mile Metropolitan Avenue line operated more or less in a straight line east and west on Grand and Metropolitan avenues from the Williamsburg Bridge plaza, on the west to the intersection of Metropolitan with Jamaica Avenue on the east. The line operated out of the Depot located at Broadway and Jamaica avenues until 1941, and Fresh Pond Depot after that. A ride over the entire line normally consumed 66 minutes.

Here we see a double-ended Peter Witt car that had been converted to a single end car, even though it retained its double-end capability. Car 8525, one of the "speed cars" (8100s and 8500s) is operating on a railfan special because this type was never operated on the Metropolitan Avenue line. Our educated guess on the location of this photo is the East Williamsburg end of the English Kills Branch of Newtown Creek drawbridge the only place single track was encountered on the long Metropolitan Avenue Line. The Metropolitan Avenue cars used Grand Street west of the drawbridge, as the Metropolitan Ave. tracks were out of service. As a footnote, July 17, 1949 marked the last use of this "speed"-type car, when the Ocean Avenue line was converted to use of the slower 8300 series and all 8100s and 8500s were scrapped, except 8111, which was sent to Branford Museum in 1952 after being hidden away, ostensibly by transit employees who were sympathetic to railfans. *(Lawson K. Hill, Boston Chapter, NRHS Collection)*

Brooklyn's Conventional Streetcars

(Above) Car 8476 is on the Metropolitan Ave. line at 69th St. Middle Village, the last full day of service, June 11, 1949.
(Everett A. White, courtesy of Don Harold)

(Below) On June 11, 1949 car 8454 was at the eastern terminal, Metropolitan Ave. at Jamaica Ave. on the last full day of service.
(Everett A. White, courtesy of Don Harold)

Brooklyn's Conventional Streetcars

Peter Witt car 8490 is on Metropolitan Avenue at Lefferts Boulevard, also on June 11, 1949.
(Everett A. White, courtesy Donald Harold)

Peter Witts 8473 and 8525 were operating as a railfan special on the Metropolitan Avenue line on March 14, 1948.
(Lawson K. Hill, Boston Chapter, NRHS Collection)

The 8525 sits astride the expressway opposite the entrance to LaGuardia Airport during the March 14, 1948 fantrip. The car was built in 1925 as a double-ender by Osgood Bradley, but was converted to single end two years later. *(Lawson K. Hill, Boston Chapter, NRHS Collection)*

Brooklyn's Conventional Streetcars

JUNCTION BOULEVARD LINE

Following the truncation of the Grand Street line to Maspeth Depot, a new line was created on the outer end, Rt. 72- Junction Boulevard. This line was notable in that it ended at the landmark LaGuardia airport in Queens originally known as North Beach Airport. The bridge over the Grand Central Parkway was the point where the cars changed ends for the return trip and is notable in that the bridge still exists today, although the airport beyond has gone through numerous changes. It was converted to bus on August 14, 1949.

The 8532 is at LaGuardia during a railfan outing on March 14, 1948.
(Lawson K. Hill, Boston Chapter, NRHS Collection)

Fantrip car 8104 was turning out of Palmetto Street onto Seneca Avenue to operate over the DeKalb Avenue line on June 19, 1949.
(Everett A. White, courtesy of Don Harold)

Brooklyn's Conventional Streetcars

The 8104 is at the same location on June 19, 1949. *(Everett A. White, coutesy Donald Harold)*

Another fantrip photo stop was made on Jackson Mill Road at Astoria Boulevard in the Corona Section of Queens on June 19, 1949. *(Everett A. White, courtesy of Don Harold)*

Brooklyn's Conventional Streetcars

The Final Peter Witt Cars

After most of the streetcar lines in Brooklyn were abandoned, PCC cars could hold down about 90% of the requirements on the three remaining lines, McDonald, Church Avenue, and Coney Island Ave. During rush hours, a small fleet of 20 Peter Witt cars, in the 8400 series plus the 8361, were retained to operate over a portion of the McDonald Ave. line between 9th Ave Depot (at 20th Street) and Avenue I. The 8361 was retained because one of the 8400 series selected had been in an accident. The 8361 is currently preserved at Kingston, NY and the 8111 is preserved at Shore Line Trolley Museum in Connecticut.

Peter Witt 8454 is operating over the private right of way used by the Smith-Coney Island Avenue cars connecting Brighton Beach Avenue with the West 5th Street trolley terminal at Coney Island. This car was on a fantrip, on July 27, 1953, since the Peter Witts never made it to Coney Island during the last few years of operation. The Brighton elevated line can be seen in the background.
(Edward S. Miller)

Brooklyn's Conventional Streetcars

Brooklyn's Conventional Streetcars

West End Bay Ridge Lines

The West End line began as the steam-operated Brooklyn, Bath and West End Railroad, was bought out by the Brooklyn Rapid Transit and electrified for use by elevated trains that were forced to operate on the surface until the elevated structure was built. Today the resulting structure is still used by the B & W-West End subway trains. The el structure did not use Bath Avenue. Instead it was built over 86th Street so the streetcars continued to serve the former el train territory. After World War II, the West End surface streetcar line was abandoned without replacement. This car, 2576, has just left the private right of way once used by the elevated trains on the surface on the West End line. It is preparing to turn left onto Bath Avenue enroute to the Ulmer Park loop on October 18, 1943. During the winter months, the West End line terminated at Ulmer Park loop on 25th Avenue. During the summer months 8000 series Peter Witts carried the large crowds on this line all the way to the Coney Island - Stillwell and Surf Avenue. It is said that older people preferred the streetcars as a means of getting to Coney Island so as to avoid climbing the stairs to the elevated platforms.

(Lawson K. Hill, Boston Chapter, NRHS Collection)

Brooklyn's Conventional Streetcars

(Above) Veteran Stephenson car 2554, dating all the way back to 1907, but rebuilt several times, sits on Surf Avenue at the entrance to Sea Gate, a gated community. The line connected that community with Coney Island Amusement Park and ended at Ocean Avenue near Sheepshead Bay. *(Lawson K. Hill, Boston Chapter, NRHS Collection)*

(Left) The Bay Ridge Avenue line like the West End (surface) line began at Ulmer Park loop and operated northwesterly via Bay Ridge Avenue to the locale of the same name at 65th Street and 3rd Avenue. Peter Witt car 8173 is on 3rd Avenue at 65th Street. This was in the general vicinity of the 58th Street Depot, from which both lines operated, located on 57th Street between 2nd and 3rd Avenue. Bay Ridge was abandoned on May 15, 1949 about the time this photo was made.
(Everett A. White, courtesy of Don Harold)

Brooklyn's Conventional Streetcars

One of the last operable Peter Witt cars in Brooklyn, 8454 was used on a fantrip on September 27, 1953. It was photographed here on Neptune Avenue near the Coney Island terminal of the McDonald and Coney Island Avenue line. *(Edward S. Miller)*

Single-end car 6013 sits at the Avenue U loop, the southern terminal of the Nostrand Ave. line, one of the longest and most heavily patronized lines in Brooklyn. Ordinarily cars on this route crossed the Williamsburg Bridge to Delancy Street, in Manhattan, but for some reason, this car is signed up BRIDGE ONLY on September 10, 1949, which meant it would turn back at the Williamsburg Bridge Plaza in Brooklyn, not usually done.
(Eugene Van Dusen)

Tillary Street loop was also the end of the Putnam Avenue line. Car 8487 was photographed there alongside Washington Street and Wood Street on September 10, 1949, which formed the eastern boundary of the huge Sands Street elevated station. It was torn down after el service was cut back to Bridge and Jay Streets in 1943. Most car lines signed Borough Hall looped here. The garage for the main Brooklyn Post Office, on Adams Street, is visible at the right of the photo. Note the DANGER sign on dash, REMOVE OTHER POLE BEFORE RAISING THIS POLE. With the advent of trolley buses in Brooklyn, some operators mistakenly put up the pole on the negative wire and the resultant short circuit caused fireworks. The rule to keep lights on at night by having one pole up, while raising the other one when changing ends was therefore rescinded in territory shared with the trolley buses, as too many nighttime dead shorts had occurred. *(Eugene Van Dusen)*

58   *Brooklyn's Conventional Streetcars*

THE DEKALB SHOPS

Peter Witt type car 6044, Osgood Bradley, 1930, is siding astride shop trucks in the yard beside De Kalb shops on March 14, 1948. It is still adorned in its original Aurora red and cream trim livery. Until 1948, turnstiles were on-board, accepting nickels, dimes and tokens issued by the operator for transfers and 3 cent half-fare for children. The seven-cent fare went into effect in 1948 and the turnstiles were removed. An old-fashioned hand-cranked farebox that accepted pennies collected the fares from that time on. The church in the background is St. Aloysius on Onderdonk Avenue. In the era of trackless trolleys, 1948-1962, wires were strung from Flushing Ave. on Onderdonk Ave. to Seneca Avenue to bring the TTs to the shop when necessary. Traction motors could only be changed out here at De Kalb, not in Bergen Street or Crosstown barns.
(Lawson K. Hill, Boston Chapter, NRHS Collection)

A damaged single-end Peter Witt, 8050, sits on shop trucks made from old Brill 39E truck frames at De Kalb Ave shops in Ridgewood. The shop was located in Ridgewood on the Brooklyn-Queens border at De Kalb and Seneca Avenues. Cars 6000-6049 were built in order to improve upon the double ended design delivered in 1924-26 in the 8000-8400 series. They had leather seats.
(Lawson K. Hill, Boston Chapter, NRHS Collection)

Brooklyn's Conventional Streetcars

The 6023 was of a group of 200 similar cars, (6000-6199, Brill, Osgood Bradley, 1930-31). The first 50 contained deep-cushioned leather seats, but the rest contained wooden slat seats resulting from vandalism experienced early on. Turnstiles enforced front entrance-center exit until 1948. This photo was taken March 14, 1948. It is rumored that an additional order for 100 similar, but double-ended cars were to be ordered, but were not because of the impending design of the PCC car and a general downturn in the economic situation of the time. *(Lawson K. Hill, Boston Chapter, NRHS Collection)*

The 8264, shown here at DeKalb Avenue shops, has apparently just received a "nose job", probably the result of a minor fender-bender accident. On March 14, 1948, the car had a few more good miles left in it, but time was running out on the nearly quarter-century old vehicle. *(Lawson K. Hill, Boston Chapter NRHS Collection)*

Brooklyn's Conventional Streetcars

The PCC Car in Brooklyn

Brooklyn was the proving ground for many of the streetcar technological innovations that were being tested by the Electric Railway Presidents' Conference Committee during the early 1930s. There were two experimental cars, one numbered 5200, built by Twin Coach, and the other numbered 5300, built by Pullman (dubbed its "Model B"). The Twin Coach car had previously operated briefly in Cleveland, while the 5300 had operated in Chicago, where it was built, as well as Cleveland before entering service in Brooklyn on October 19, 1934. The two experimental cars operated primarily on the Flatbush Avenue line.

Thus it was no surprise that Brooklyn and Queens Transit became the first property to order the final PCC product, when it was finally made available. In June 1935 one all-aluminum car was ordered from the Clark Equipment Company and 99 cars were ordered from St. Louis Car Company, a veteran car builder. Most of the 100 cars were delivered in the summer of 1936 and entered service ceremoniously on October 1st of that year. The 1000 was delivered in early 1937 and soon joined the others in service. All 100 cars rode on Clark trucks.

The cars were financed through the Brooklyn Trust Company, who wanted to have a say in how the cars were treated while in service. The bank insisted that the cars be stored indoors when not in service and the 9th Avenue Depot was the chosen carhouse. B&QT would have preferred to operate the cars on Flatbush Avenue, but that would have put an undue amount of non-revenue mileage on the cars, or caused them to be stored out of doors. So the first 100 (and as it turned out, the only) PCC cars were assigned to the 28- Erie Basin, 67- Seventh Avenue, 68- Smith St.-Coney Island, and 69- McDonald – Vanderbilt lines. The Erie Basin, Seventh Avenue and McDonald –Vanderbilt car lines operated over the Brooklyn Bridge to an under-the-elevated loop at Park Row in Manhattan.

Largely as a result of the immense popularity of the PCC cars with the riding public, and, as a job creation measure the Reconstruction Finance Corporation, in 1937, was willing to fund an additional 500 PCC cars. They would have extensively modernized the streetcar system in Brooklyn, including the Flatbush Avenue lines. This, of course would entail the outdoor storage of the new cars, but the reason that the cars were never ordered, or built, is because Mayor Fiorello LaGuardia, the same mayor who'd had his picture taken at the inaugural run less than a year before, put a stop to all further streetcar construction or line modernization in New York City. That included the Third Avenue Railway as well as the Brooklyn and Queens Transit System. This stance was never rescinded, and only World War II's intervention prevented a premature massive bus substitution program across the city of New York.

For a period of two days, April 30, and May 1, 1939, PCC cars operated on a trial basis between Boro Hall and the World's Fair Grounds in Flushing Meadows, Queens, via the Gates Avenue and Flushing Ridgewood lines during the fair dedication ceremonies.

When the fair opened, in May 1939, only regular Flushing-Ridgewood cars served the fair and the PCCs reverted to their normal routes.

The prevailing four line pattern of PCC operation continued from October 1936, with minor changes, until March 1940, when the Erie Basin line coverage was reverted to older 4100 series cars, freeing up additional PCCs for the other three lines.

In 1944, at the height of World War II, the elevated line over the Brooklyn Bridge was abandoned and PCC cars on the 7th Avenue line as well as other lines were operated into Manhattan on newly constructed trackage connecting to the el tracks, to a new surface seven-tracked streetcar terminal at Park Row. At the end of the war, Mayor LaGuardia's grand streetcar conversion plan was again put into play and massive line abandonments ensued, including two of the PCC lines. On June 17, 1946, the Smith Street portion of the Smith-Coney Island Avenue line was discontinued due to the rebuilding of the 9th Street bridge over the Gowanus Canal. Streetcars operated only south of Bartel-Pritchard Square. Then on September 22, 1946, the Smith-Coney Island Avenue line was officially renamed the 68- Coney Island Ave. line.

Because the handwriting was on the wall for the demise of streetcar service in Brooklyn, the B&QT advertised the 15 oldest PCCs for sale in January 1950. In anticipation of their sale, they were withdrawn from service, only to be put back into service at the end of the year, because there were no offers to purchase them. On August 1, 1950, the 69- McDonald-Vanderbilt line was split into two parts, with the Vanderbilt portion being converted to bus. PCC cars continued to serve the southern portion of the line, from 9th Ave. Depot to Coney Island. Then on February 11, 1951, the Seventh Avenue line was converted to bus, thus ending all PCC operation into Manhattan.

As other streetcar lines using older cars were one by one given the ax, the PCC lines were retained because the financing arrangements on the cars called for a 20-year life span. Whereas throughout the years, the older Peter Witt cars in the 6000 and 8000 series had helped out on the PCC lines, as the patronage dwindled and the PCC lines shrunk, with few exceptions only the PCC cars remained. Coinciding with the February 11, 1951 abandonment of the Seventh Avenue line, the 35- Church Ave. crosstown line was converted to PCC operation. This allowed scrapping of all, but a handful of the 8400 series Peter Witts which were retained to operate on the McDonald Ave. line during rush hours between McDonald Ave./20th Street and Avenue I. The last use of these cars in rush hour service was on November 1, 1954.

Most of the 100 car fleet of PCCs soldiered on until their 20th birthday, which was October 1, 1956. Because parts were in short supply and the number of serviceable cars was dwindling, the Coney Island Avenue line was abandoned on November 30, 1955. Thirty-one days past the 20th anniversary of PCC operation in Brooklyn, on October 31, 1956, the last cars were operated on Church and McDonald Avenues, thus ending over 60 years of streetcar service. It is hard to believe that the streetcars have been gone for almost as long as they had operated!

Only two Brooklyn PCC cars were saved from scrapping. The 1000 today resides at the Trolley Museum of New York in Kingston, New York, and the 1001 operates at the Shoreline Trolley Museum in Branford, Connecticut.

Car 1012 on a fantrip at Ulmer Park loop of the West End line on November 24, 1946. This car was painted in an experimental "Aurora" red with yellow and grey trim. It ran with that paint scheme (nicknamed "The Pink Lady") from February to December 1946, at which time the City chose the green and silver scheme as seen on the 1003 to be the standard for the fleet.
(Everett A. White, courtesy of D.W. Harold)

(Left) The original PCC, 1000 is seen entering the West 5th Street terminal at Coney Island on May 15, 1955. This was the only trolley built by Clark Equipment Company and was of all aluminum construction, as opposed to the steel construction of the remainder of the fleet. By the time this photo was taken, the front end panels had been rebuilt to more closely resemble the St. Louis Car Company version because the original configuration resulted in a blind spot for the motorman, making him unable to see pedestrians crossing in front of the car. *(Frank Pfuhler)*

(Right) The first PCC car to be repainted into the then experimental green and silver paint scheme, car 1003 (nicknamed "The Green Hornet") is seen entering the Park Row terminal in Manhattan in June 1946. Sister car 1012 was painted an experimental red color at the same time and the 1003's scheme was ultimately chosen to be standard for streetcars, trolley coaches, and buses.
(Everett A. White, courtesy of Don Harold)

CAR 1000 "CANHEAD"

(Above) A rear view of 1000 on Church Avenue displays the design that would be copied on the postwar variations of the PCC car. Photo was taken August 31, 1953.
(Lawson K. Hill, Boston Chapter, NRHS Collection)

(Left) Running out its last days on the Church Avenue line, the 1000 passes Bedford Ave. eastbound towards the Bristol Street loop on January 27, 1956.
(Walter E. Zullig)

The B&QT 1000 was Brooklyn's first PCC car and the only PCC ever built entirely of aluminum by the Clark Equipment Company. It was delivered in the Spring of 1937 as the 100th PCC car, and placed into service shortly thereafter. The inaugural run of the other PCC cars had been on October 1, 1936. During its early years, the car was not liked by motormen because there was a blind spot in the lower left hand corner of the windshield that prevented him from viewing pedestrians crossing in front of the car without standing up from the seat. In the early 1940s the car was involved in an accident that required the entire front of the car to be replaced. At that time a standard PCC car front was grafted onto the car thereby endearing it to the motormen.

The standee window arrangement proved to be a forerunner of the postwar designs put out by St. Louis Car Company and Pullman Standard, but the aluminum products of Clark were never duplicated.

The BQT employees often referred to the 1000 as the "Queen Mary", but the railfans preferred to call it "Canhead" after the popular Dick Tracy character of the time.

After many false starts, the car is currently being preserved at the Trolley Museum of New York in Kingston.

63

(Above) A view of the left side of car 1000 as seen on Church Avenue approaching the intersection of McDonald Avenue on January 27, 1956. Whereas the other cars were in rather rag-tag condition at this late date, the 1000 appears to be pretty well preserved. It would go on to achieve museum status at the Trolley Museum of New York, following retirement. *(Walter E. Zullig)*

(Below) This view 1000 operating on Church Avenue on August 31, 1953 emphasizes the Brooklyn practice of delineating the final destination of the car with a red headsign background.
(Lawson K. Hill, Boston Chapter, NRHS Collection)

PCCs In The Early Years

When delivered, the PCC cars were painted in what would appear to be a tan color with a red stripe around the belt rail. Native Brooklynites will tell you that the color was officially called Dupont Cordova Gray and the belt rail was painted Mountain Laurel Scarlet with no apologies to the Lehigh Valley Transit, where that same color (called Mountain Ash Scarlet in PA) was also coming into vogue in the late 1930s. Over the headlight in the center of the dash there was a red light that could be lit when the passenger load had reached capacity and the following car was close at hand. The light being lit indicated to would be passengers that this car would discharge only, so that the car could catch up to its schedule, and thereby speed all passengers' rides. Apparently during the first rebuilding of the cars, this light was removed, probably because nobody paid any attention to it or they didn't understand what it was intended to indicate. Some of the 6000 series Peter Witts had a glass window in the front that read "car full" only when the light behind it was lit. The photo below shows car 1013 operating in the original B&QT scheme on the McDonald-Vanderbilt line passing the 9th Avenue Depot. Time frame would be about the end of World War II. *(R. Fillman)*

Car 1003 in a brand new paint scheme is seen operating on the Seventh Avenue line in October 1946. This was the first car to be painted green and silver, having received that treatment in June 1946 on a trial basis. At the same time car 1012 was painted red with gray and yellow trim and four buses were repainted various colors including one which was green and silver. The public voted for the green and silver and on December 24, 1946 that scheme was adopted as the standard that would endure to the end of electrified surface transit in Brooklyn.
(Everett White, courtesy of Don Harold)

65

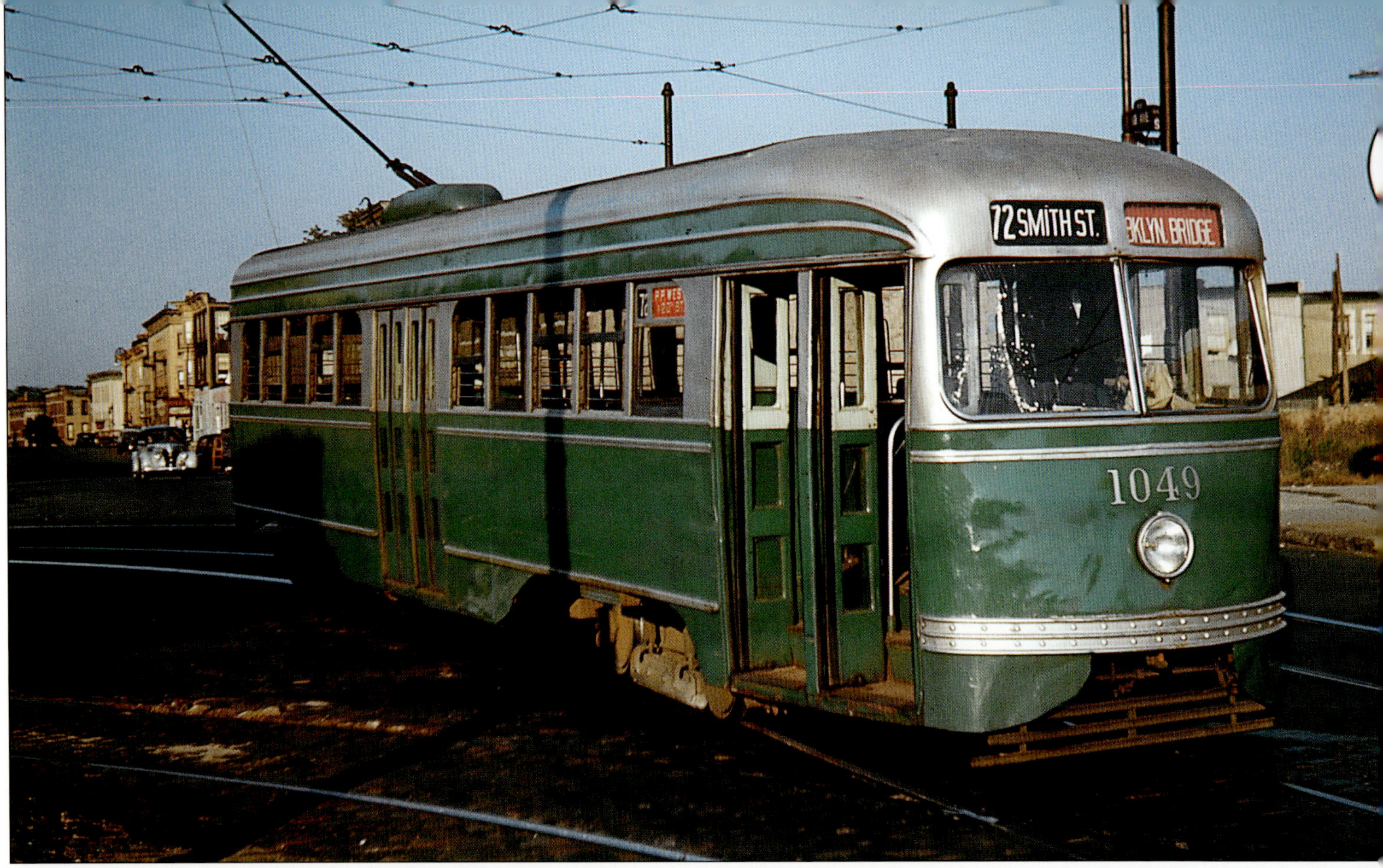
72 SMITH ST.
BKLYN. BRIDGE
1049

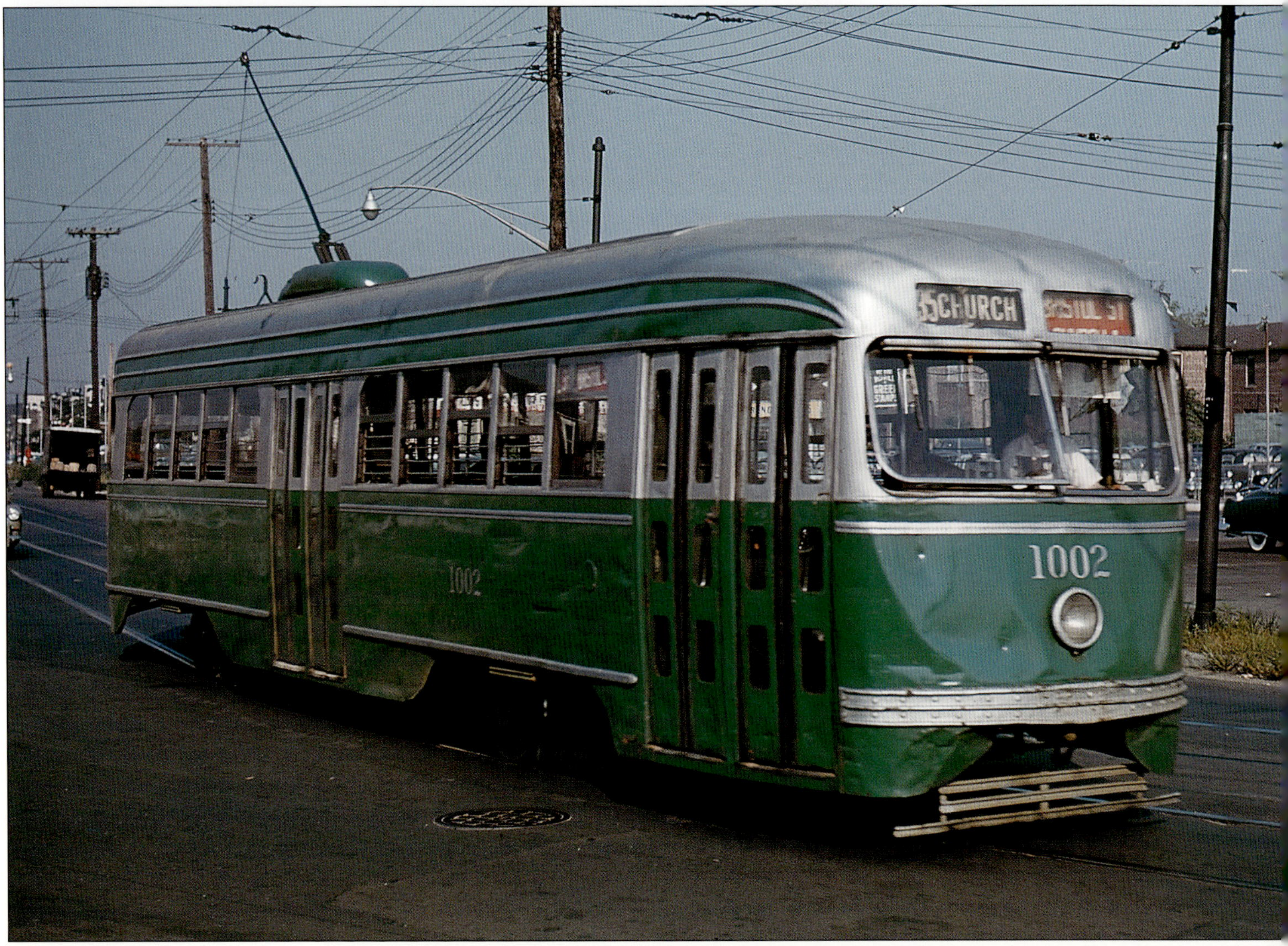
CHURCH
1002
1002

(Left) PCC 1049 is signed up for Rt. "72" - Smith St. while laying over beside the Ninth Avenue Depot. Since the Smith – Coney Island line was route 75, the author learned, upon investigation, that about 20 PCCs had erroneous head signs that were later corrected. However, the side signs were never changed and after February 11, 1951 the line was converted to bus so there was no need for the correction. The photo dates from the late 1940s as the trackage over the Brooklyn Bridge was closed down for bridge repairs on March 5, 1950, never to be reopened. Prior to April 30, 1949 the northern end of the line on Smith Street was also temporarily converted to buses due to bridge reconstruction over the Gowanus Canal. *(Frank Watson)*

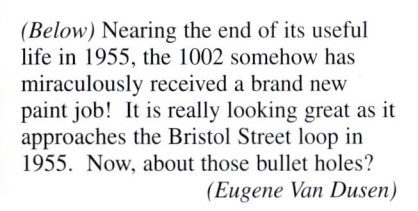

(Above) Ninth Avenue Depot represented the last bastion of streetcar operating maintenance depots in Brooklyn. The unusual ventilatored 1010 and 1080 are on the ready tracks on May 15, 1955. The 1010 would be used by railfan that particular day. *(Frank Pfuhler)*

(Below) Nearing the end of its useful life in 1955, the 1002 somehow has miraculously received a brand new paint job! It is really looking great as it approaches the Bristol Street loop in 1955. Now, about those bullet holes?
(Eugene Van Dusen)

PCC Lines in Brooklyn

During the last few years of trolley operation in Brooklyn, there were only three lines left operating and all base service was provided exclusively by the 100 PCC cars, now 15 years old. Because the city was obligated to operate the PCCs at least 20 years, and the city wanted to rid the streets of rail lines, the cars received little in the way of cosmetic attention. Rush hour service was provided over a portion of the McDonald Ave. line to Avenue I, a crossover, which required the use of double ended cars. Some 8400 series Peter Witt cars, were used in the service up until November 1, 1954 when the use of these cars was discontinued, making Brooklyn a 100% PCC venue.

McDonald Avenue Line

The McDonald Avenue line operated from the Ninth Avenue Depot on the north, straight south along McDonald Avenue eleven miles, to a terminal on West Fifth Street at Coney Island. From Ninth Ave. to just south of the intersection of another PCC line, Church Avenue, the street was a wide, uncluttered thoroughfare. Then just south of Church Avenue, at Ditmas and McDonald, the tracks ran beneath the elevated structure of the BMT, later the IND Culver Line. For a portion of the way, the PCC cars shared rails with the freight trains of the South Brooklyn Railway. What follows here are several scenes taken along the line during the period from 1951 to the line's abandonment on October 31, 1956. No bus substitution was made for the streetcars on this route.

McDonald Avenue Line - Brooklyn

McDonald Avenue Line - Brooklyn

Brooklyn's last major trolley intersection was the crossing of McDonald Ave. tracks by the Church Avenue line. Here westbound car 1020 clatters over the specialwork during June 1956. The east-to-south connectors allowed short turn cars to loop at 16th & McDonald as well as to pull in to the Ninth Avenue Depot. *(Al Holtz)*

McDonald Avenue Line - Brooklyn

(Right) Southbound PCC 1074 makes the stop at Church Avenue on September 27, 1953. Downstairs, at that time, was the termination point for the Independent subway line from Manhattan to Brooklyn. The following year it was connected to the old BMT Culver elevated line and Independent subway service was extended to Coney Island. Prior to that event, the Independent was 99% built underground.
(Edward S. Miller)

(Left) 1056 follows the 1024 at Prospect Park West and 19th Street which was the north end of the McDonald Avenue car line and near the 9th Ave. Depot. September 27, 1953. *(Edward S. Miller)*

(Below) Just below Avenue C, the subway-to-elevated connection on McDonald Avenue can be seen. The excavation and construction for this connection was begun in 1941 and finished shortly after the war's end. However, the actual through service by the IND to Coney Island did not commence until 1954. Car 1037 is northbound on McDonald skirting the subway portal on April 21, 1956.
(Edward S. Miller)

McDonald Avenue Line - Brooklyn

McDonald Avenue Line - Brooklyn

Car 1022 is southbound on McDonald Avenue making the stop at Church Avenue on September 5, 1956, less than two months prior to abandonment.
(J.M. Canfield)

McDonald Avenue Line - Brooklyn

(Right) Three PCC cars are stacked up on the short stretch of private right of way on McDonald Ave. at Cortelyou Road. The date is May 15, 1955. There has undoubtedly been some sort of an obstruction on the line that is impeding the streetcar flow, as witness the police cars, two TA and one unmarked. Cortelyou Road had electric buses which accounts for the double wires in the foreground. *(Frank Pfuhler)*

(Below) PCC 1010, the only car with the roof top ventilator, is seen at the 16th Ave. loop on McDonald Ave., May 15, 1955. *(Frank Pfuhler)*

(Left) 1019 is on the 16th Avenue short turn loop for cars coming off of the Church Avenue line onto McDonald for a few blocks' run south on McDonald. The loop was near Corteylou Road, a street made famous as a proving ground for the trolleybus concept in Brooklyn beginning in 1930 was formerly the southern terminal for the Gravesend-Church Avenue line which used the single ended 6000 series Peter Witt cars. Prior to the 1930s, Gravesend was the name of the street that became McDonald Avenue. The BQT never got around the changing their destination signs accordingly. The photo was taken April 21, 1956.

(Edward S. Miller)

Kensington Junction was the location where the South Brooklyn Railway rails joined the McDonald Avenue car line. The Culver elevated tracks are overhead as the 1047 proceeds southbound on McDonald with Cortelyou Road in the background. *(Frank Pfuhler)*

Car 1065 is southbound on McDonald Ave. south of Ditmas Avenue on October 21, 1956, where the South Brooklyn Railway tracks joined the streetcars underneath the elevated structure.

(Frank Pfuhler)

McDonald Avenue Line - Brooklyn

Car 1010 is shown on McDonald at Avenue P on May 15, 1955. *(Frank Pfuhler)*

Avenue Z is where the South Brooklyn Railway had a small yard that services the huge New York City Transit Authority Coney Island rapid transit shop complex. The 1075 is at that location on August 19, 1956. *(Frank Pfuhler)*

McDonald Avenue Line - Brooklyn

(Left) Car 1074 is approaching the Coney Island, i.e. southern, terminal of the McDonald Avenue line on September 27, 1953. It is leaving private right of way at what was formerly the Culver Terminal (i.e. before the el was built) and is about to enter the wooden trolley terminal building on West 5th Street. The track coming in from the right was used by cars arriving from the Coney Island Avenue line that also used the terminal. The elevated structure in the background is the Culver line merging in with the lower level to its Stillwell Avenue terminal.

(Edward S. Miller)

McDonald Avenue Line - Brooklyn

(Avove) Fantrip car 1010 entering the W. 5th Street loop at Coney Island Ave. on May 15, 1955. *(Frank Pfuhler)*

(Left) McDonald Avenue car 1021 is operating on West 5th Street at Seabreeze Avenue. A right turn here leads to the Coney Island Avenue line while straight ahead leads to McDonald. The date was September 27, 1953.
(Edward S. Miller)

(Left) It was rather dark inside the W. 5th Street Coney Island trolley terminal so photography there was difficult at best. The 1079 rests there on May 21, 1951. *(Eugene Van Dusen)*

McDonald Avenue Line - Brooklyn

Coney Island Avenue Line

(Above) About a week prior to the end of service on Coney Island Avenue, in November 1955, car 1022 loads up at Bartel-Pritchard Square for the long trek south across Brooklyn. *(Al Holtz)*

(Below) Southbound car 1002 on the Coney Island Avenue car line is on Prospect Park Southwest. The red sign on the span wire states "Section insulator, shut off power". The presence of multiple feeder cables indicates that this is a power division point. *(Edward S. Miller)*

The 11.5 mile Coney Island Avenue line paralleled the McDonald Ave route several blocks to the east. As the Smith-Coney Island Avenue line it had the honor of becoming the first totally PCC-equipped line in Brooklyn, on November 7, 1936. Then on September 22, 1946, the Smith Street line which formed the northern portion of the route, was converted to buses, and the latter day Coney Island line continued on with PCCs for nine more years. As such the line began at Bartel-Pritchard Square where there was some non-revenue connecting track over Prospect Park West to the Ninth Avenue Depot. The line ran straight as an arrow south to a point just south of the Belt Parkway overpass where it turned onto Brighton Avenue, then Sea Breeze Ave. for the short run to the Coney Island streetcar terminal. The line was converted to buses on November 30, 1955, almost a year before the remainder of the system closed.

Coney Island Avenue Line - Brooklyn

A 1949 Chevy "spoils" an otherwise nice shot of PCC 1083 on Coney Island Avenue at 16th Street.
(Frank Pfuhler)

Brooklyn's only limited access highway at that time was the Belt Parkway that was constructed in the late 1930s parallel to the southern extremity of the Borough. Here we see an unidentified PCC crossing over the parkway on September 25, 1955. *(Frank Pfuhler)*

Another view at the same location on the same day.
(Frank Pfuhler)

Coney Island Avenue Line - Brooklyn

Coney Island Avenue Line - Brooklyn

PCCs 1018 and 1038 pass on Prospect Park Southwest at Bartel-Pritchard Square. The square provided a loop at the north end of the Coney Island Ave. line. September 27, 1953. *(Edward S. Miller)*

Coney Island Avenue Line - Brooklyn

Two PCCs, 1055 and 1028 are seen on Coney Island Avenue at Kings Highway on July 4, 1955. The concrete safety islands, shown here, were the nemesis of auto drivers everywhere in the US where streetcars operated in the center of wide thoroughfares. *(Frank Pfuhler)*

Coney Island Avenue Line - Brooklyn

1022 is eastbound on Seabreeze Avenue at West 3rd Street on October 21, 1955.
(J.M. Canfield)

(Above) 1002 is on West 5th Street at Seabreeze Avenue near the Coney Island terminal. The car will turn right at this point to continue its journey up Coney Island Avenue to Bartel-Pritchard Square on September 27, 1953. *(Edward S. Miller)*

(Below) Car 1043 is nearing the end of its journey to Coney Island on Seabreeze Avenue at the corner of West 5th Street on September 27, 1953. *(Edward S. Miller)*

PCC 1052 is on West 5th Street entering the Coney Island terminal area on September 27, 1953. *(Edward S. Miller)*

Coney Island Avenue Line - Brooklyn

Coney Island Ave. car 1080 is operating over the private right-of-way connecting Brighton Beach Avenue with Sea Breeze Avenue. Overhead on the elevated structure a former 200 series el trailer, now used as a crew room can be seen.
(Frank Pfuhler)

The original PCC, the 1000, is exiting the Coney Island terminal on the Coney Island Ave. line, May 15, 1955.
(Frank Pfuhler)

PCC 1000 is seen from the rear, leaving the Coney Island terminal on May 15, 1955.
(Frank Pfuhler)

Coney Island Avenue Line - Brooklyn

Church Avenue Line

On February 11, 1951, the PCC Seventh Avenue line was converted to bus and at that time there were enough surplus PCCs to allow retirement of the remaining 6000 series Peter Witt cars and made Brooklyn an all PCC property for base service. The Church Avenue line during the PCC era was a combination of two routes. Route 8- Church Avenue operated Canarsie to 39th St. Ferry and Route 13 Gravesend-Church duplicated the eastern end of the line, turning south on McDonald to 16th Avenue which was discontinued. The resulting line was renumbered 35- Church Ave. The line began at the Canarsie Depot on the east end of town and operated due west past Coney Island Avenue, crossed under the intersection of Ocean Parkway in a short subway private right-of-way, crossed McDonald Avenue and proceeded over 39th Street to a loop near the Brooklyn waterfront at 39th Street and First Avenue. This area was shared with the South Brooklyn Railway yards and was the site of a Ferry Terminal that was abandoned in the early 1930s. The line was one of the last two car lines in Brooklyn, being converted to bus on October 31, 1956.

The 1044 is at Bristol Street terminal, the extreme eastern point of the Church Avenue line, September 21, 1956.
(Walter E. Zullig)

Cars 1000 and 1080 are at the Bristol Street loop near Hegeman Avenue, September 27, 1953.
(Edward S. Miller)

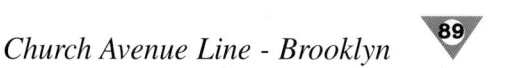

Church Avenue Line - Brooklyn

89

The original Clark Equipment Co. PCC 1000 is at Bristol Street loop on May 13, 1956.
(Eugene Van Dusen)

Car 1044 at the Bristol Street loop on January 27, 1956. *(Walter E. Zullig)*

1006 at Bristol Street loop, August 31, 1953. *(Lawson K. Hill, Boston Chapter, NRHS Collection)*

1038 at Bristol Street loop, August 31, 1953. *(Lawson K. Hill, Boston Chapter, NRHS Collection)*

1085 at Bristol Street loop, September 27, 1953. *(Edward S. Miller)*

Church Avenue Line - Brooklyn

Church Avenue Line - Brooklyn

(Left) Battered but still running with only a few months to go to retirement. PCC car 1021 is on Church Avenue in East Flatbush, probably in the neighborhood of New York and Utica avenues. This was a very busy crosstown line, always a car in sight. When buses came, business declined so more auto traffic and fewer parking spaces became the norm.
(Frank Pfuhler)

(Below) The 1001 is westbound emerging from the underpass under Ocean Parkway in January 1956. This car would later be preserved at the Shore Line Museum, East Haven, Conn. *(Al Holtz)*

Fantrip car 1010 is eastbound on Church Avenue at East 5th Street, about to duck under Ocean Parkway. May 15, 1955. *(Frank Pfuhler)*

Car 1010 is in the underpass on the private right of way. May 15, 1955. *(Frank Pfuhler)*

94

Church Avenue Line - Brooklyn

Car 1039 is crossing Coney Island Avenue on the Church Ave. line in January 1956. *(Al Holtz)*

The 1010 is emerging from the underpass under Ocean Parkway on the Church Avenue line, May 15, 1955. *(Frank Pfuhler)*

Church Avenue Line - Brooklyn

Car 1000 is on Church Avenue August 31, 1953. *(Lawson K. Hill, Boston Chapter, NRHS Collection)*

The 1030 is on Church Avenue near McDonald on September 6, 1955. *(Walter E. Zullig)*

96 *Church Avenue Line - Brooklyn*

The 1092 is on a short stretch of narrow street transitioning from Church Avenue onto 37th Street, September 27, 1953. *(Edward S. Miller)*

The Church Avenue line made about a two block jog west of McDonald where it crossed the tracks of the South Brooklyn Railroad at grade and passed under the Culver elevated line at the same time. The 1063 is eastbound on the Church Ave. line on 13th Avenue and is about to turn onto 37th Street on September 27, 1953. About two blocks later it will be on Church Ave. Note the DANGER-STOP sign hanging from the elevated structure. (The word "CROSSING" has broken off of this sign) Also the trolley wire in troughs for the trolley operated South Brooklyn electric locomotives. This was a very sharp and tight curve for the trolleys and one of the few points in all of Brooklyn where the cars could not pass one another on a curve. Red signs hung from the span wires warning the motormen of this fact. The car line ran for two blocks on 13th Avenue and then turned right to 39th Street. *(Edward S. Miller)*

Near the far western end of the Church Ave. line, car 1083 is about to turn east into 39th Street at the beginning of its trek to Canarsie Depot and Bristol Street loop. The tracks on 2nd Ave. are freight only. South Brooklyn and Bush Terminal railroads used them. Originally, trolleys did not use the freight tracks but went to a stub end terminal at the 39th Street ferry. With the advent of the 6000 series single-enders in 1931, two South Brooklyn freight tracks were used to take the cars to a new loop at 1st Ave., since that time the ferry itself has been abandoned. The 8th Ave. line also used this loop. Operators had to be extra careful here as the switches were double-tongued and if a freight had passed the operator had to get out the switch iron and be certain to throw both tongues. Photo was taken September 27, 1953.
(Edward S. Miller)

97

Church Avenue Line - Brooklyn

The 004 operates on the short stretch of private right-of-way leading to the 39th Street Ferry loop on March 19, 1955. *(Frank Pfuhler)*

98   *Church Avenue Line - Brooklyn*

The 1073 is on the 1st Avenue loop marking the western end of the Church Avenue line on July 21, 1955.
(Walter E. Zullig)

The Trolley Coach in Brooklyn

It was only a natural evolution in the history of electric traction in Brooklyn that trolley coaches should be tried out. After all, the city had an absolutely huge investment in direct current traction power-generation equipment in the 1920s with dozens of subway lines, over seventy streetcar lines, hundreds upon hundreds of subway cars, and even electrified trolley freight service. Indeed, many hotels and businesses in the city were wired for D.C. current. The state of the art in gasoline buses of the day left a lot to be desired as well, with the constant requirement for the driver to be shifting gears while making change, collecting fares, and handling transfers.

So, on July 23, 1930, the Brooklyn and Queens Transit Corporation inaugurated a test line on Cortelyou Road between Flatbush Avenue and Coney Island Ave. using two electric buses, as they came to be referred to in Brooklyn, and one gas bus used for comparison purposes. Two years later, the line was extended from Coney Island Ave. to the 62nd St. and New Utrecht Avenue elevated station along Dahill Road, 16th Avenue and 62nd Street. Additional coaches were purchased, and the 23 line was named the Cortelyou Road line.

Whereas, the line was moderately successful for a light feeder line to the elevated system, PCC cars were chosen to modernize the car lines. In 1936 100 PCC cars were purchased to equip four major lines, 28, 67, 68 and 69. However, ridership increased so dramatically on the four lines that the PCC cars had to be removed from the 28-Erie Basin line in early 1940, in order to provide additional service on the remaining three lines. No serious consideration was given to converting the heavier car lines to electric bus until after World War II when Mayor LaGuardia was on a very anti-streetcar kick and mandated that no further purchases of electric rail cars of any stripe would be forthcoming for New York City.

A grandiose plan was devised to convert a total of 14 car lines to electric bus which, if carried out, would have required the purchase of 435 coaches. After a single order for 200 St. Louis Car Company coaches were delivered and six streetcar lines were converted, the decision was made to convert all future lines to diesel bus. This was due in large part to improved designs in diesel buses, coupled with the aging overhead line infrastructure that typified the streetcar lines. Streetcar lines converted to electric bus were, in order of their appearance, 45- St. Johns Place, on September 16, 1948, 65- Bergen Street, on October 17, 1948, , 47- Tompkins Avenue on November 19, 1948, 48-Lorimer Street on March 23, 1949, 57-Flushing Avenue on November 14, 1949, and finally, 62- Graham Avenue on December 11, 1949. Lines considered for conversion, but never done were the 49- Ocean Ave., 53- Metropolitan Ave., 58- Corona Ave., 59- Grand Street, 63- 5th Avenue, 69- Vanderbuilt Avenue, and 72- Junction Boulevard.

The era of electric buses in Brooklyn lasted for only a single generation of equipment. By the time the initial fleet was worn out and in need of replacement, the infrastructure was also in need of replacement. Electric buses, being the minority mode for many years, induced the requirement that they not be replaced in-kind. The first electric bus abandonment proved to be only temporary when in 1952, the 23-Cortelyou operation (always isolated from the remainder of the system) was converted to diesels. Service was restored to electric on January 6, 1954 and was again discontinued the same day that streetcar operation in Brooklyn ceased, October 31, 1956. On May 1, 1954 construction of a housing project in East New York resulted in the early abandonment of the St. John's Place line between Ralph Ave and Pennsylvania Ave. On September 22, 1954, a small portion of the western end of the 62-Graham line was abandoned from Box Street to Long Island City. The St. John's Place line was completely abandoned on March 25, 1959 and the remaining five lines were de-electrified on July 27, 1960, ending all electrified street surface transportation in New York City.

A regular Route 57-Flushing Avenue trolley coach number 3076, bound for Civic Center stops to pick up rail fans who have gotten off a Long Island RDC fantrip at the only grade crossing in Queens of the old main line to Long Island City. By this time, March 28, 1958, the line was mostly freight, there being only two passenger trains from Oyster Bay in the morning and two back in the evening. The LI only owned two RDC cars. They were purchased to try out a new service from Babylon to Southampton during the off-peak hours. When this service did not work out, they were also tried unsuccessfully on Oyster Bay and Babylon to Patchogue off-peak runs. Consequently, they were used mostly for fantrips over non-electrified lines such as this one. The cars even proved unpopular on fantrips because of the fumes inside the cars. When streetcars operated along Flushing Ave., (it too was called the 57-Flushing Ave. car line) there were derails used at this point controlled by the Long Island block operator on duty. This scene is today obliterated, thanks to a grade crossing separation project at this location. *(Al Holtz)*

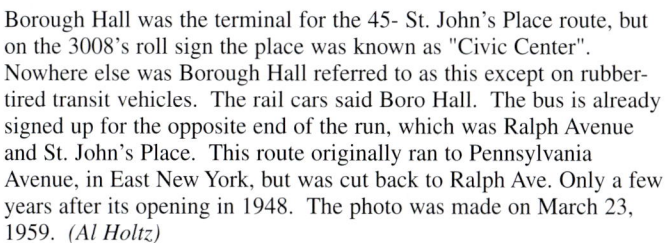

Borough Hall was the terminal for the 45- St. John's Place route, but on the 3008's roll sign the place was known as "Civic Center". Nowhere else was Borough Hall referred to as this except on rubber-tired transit vehicles. The rail cars said Boro Hall. The bus is already signed up for the opposite end of the run, which was Ralph Avenue and St. John's Place. This route originally ran to Pennsylvania Avenue, in East New York, but was cut back to Ralph Ave. Only a few years after its opening in 1948. The photo was made on March 23, 1959. *(Al Holtz)*

Brooklyn and Queens Transit began trolley coach operation on July 23, 1930 with the conversion of a portion of the 23- Corteylou Road route that operated between Flatbush Avenue and Coney Island Ave,. It was later extended over 16th Avenue to the 62nd Street and New Utrecht Ave. elevated station, and the vehicles came to be known as "electric buses" in the Brooklyn vernacular. At the peak of operation in 1956, there were seven electric bus routes. During the late 1950s they were de-emphasized and gradually phased out until the last route was converted to diesel bus in July, 1961.

The initial electric bus route was never physically connected to the postwar system.

Brooklyn Electric Buses

Brooklyn Electric Buses

The 48- Lorimer electric bus route was essentially the combination of three streetcar lines, after the streetcars were abandoned. The Franklin, Nassau and Lorimer car lines became the "Loymer", as it is pronounced in Brooklyn, route. Coach 3091 is passing Ebbetts Field on Empire Boulevard (originally called Malbone Street) just after the move of the Dodgers to Los Angeles. Demolition of Ebbetts field had begun two months earlier on February 23rd. As every reader of this book must be aware, the baseball team derived its name from the "Trolley Dodgers" who came to the games at this location. The date for the photo was April 16, 1960 and within two months, trolley coaches, like the Dodgers would be a part of Brooklyn history.
(Ray McMurdo, Bill Volkmer Collection)

Brooklyn Electric Buses

Bound for Borough Hall on July 25, 1960, two days prior to total trolley coach abandonment in Brooklyn, St. Louis-built electric bus 3056, (as trolley coaches were called in Brooklyn) operates over Flushing Avenue on the 57- Flushing Avenue route. Just behind the photographer is the intersection where the Graham Avenue route diverged. One can note the thin pavement over the streetcar tracks below. Following the demise of the electric buses, the car tracks were removed from the street.
(Joseph P. Saitta, Bill Volkmer Collection)

> Streetcar line 2- Bergen Street was abandoned on July 20, 1947 and became electric bus route 65- Bergen Street. It operated from the Brooklyn waterfront (Hamilton Ferry) over Bergen Street to Ralph Ave. and St. John's Place.

Brooklyn Electric Buses

Streetcar line 5- St. John's Place was abandoned August 24, 1947 and became electric bus route 45- St. John's Place. It originally operated from Boro Hall (a.k.a Civic Center) to Liberty and Pennsylvania Avenues. It was later cut back to Ralph Ave. and St. John's Place.

Coach 3018 is at Ralph Ave. and St. Johns Place on August 4, 1959.
(Joseph P. Saitta, Bill Volkmer Collection)

Brooklyn Electric Buses

The 3004 is passing the Long Island Rail Road station on Flatbush Avenue, on the St. John's Place route. It will soon make a left turn into Atlantic Avenue on a hot June day in 1954. *(Al Holtz)*

Brooklyn Electric Buses

Borough Hall was the western terminal for the Rt. 45 electric bus route. St. Louis-built 3008 lays over at that point on March 23, 1959, the next to last full day of electric operation on that route. *(Al Holtz)*

ROUTE 47 – THOMPKINS AVENUE

Brooklyn Electric Buses

Ebbetts Field forms a backdrop for the complex intersection of Empire Blvd., Flatbush, Washington and Ocean Avenues. This area also served as the turning loop for the Rt. 47 – Tompkins Ave. electric buses. 3137 is about to turn left off Empire onto the loop, on May 31, 1958.
(Joseph P. Saitta, Bill Volkmer Collection)

Streetcar line 7 Tompkins Avenue was abandoned August 24, 1947 and became electric bus route 47-Tompkins Ave. from Empire Blvd., (Prospect Park) and Flatbush Ave. to the Williamsburg Bridge Plaza.

Brooklyn Electric Buses

St. Louis coach 3024 on Rt. 47 approaches the Williamsburg Bridge Plaza on May 31, 1958. *(Joseph P. Saitta, Bill Volkmer Collection)*

Williamsburg Bridge Plaza served as the northern terminus for the Rt. 47- Tompkins Ave. electric bus route. Coach 3150 lays over in the shadow of the elevated structure at that point on May 31, 1958. *(Joseph P. Saitta, Bill Volkmer Collection)*

Brooklyn Electric Buses

The characteristic small windows of coach 3115 identify it as a product of St. Louis Car Co. post war production. It plies Flushing Ave. in the Williamsburg section of Brooklyn on May 31, 1958.
(Joseph P. Saitta, Bill Volkmer Collection)

The 3135 makes its initial turn from Gold onto Sands Street near the Brooklyn Bridge beginning its run over the Rt. 57- Flushing Avenue line on July 25, 1960. The next day all electrified surface transportation in New York City would end.
(Joseph P. Saitta, Bill Volkmer Collection)

ROUTE 57 - FLUSHING AVENUE

Streetcar line 57- Flushing Avenue was abandoned on November 21, 1948. It operated from the Brooklyn Bridge (Tillary Street) to Maspeth Depot, located at Grand Avenue and 69th Street, Queens.

The intersection of Flushing and Grand Ave. sees 3150, one of 200 identical electric buses operating in Brooklyn, on March 22, 1960. *(Joseph P. Saitta, Bill Volkmer Collection)*

Brooklyn Electric Buses 11

3
The South Brooklyn Railway

In the early years of subway and elevated railway construction in New York, most of the heavy materials and rail cars were delivered to the area on barges and ships. For Brooklyn, this meant that the goods were dropped off on the waterfront facing Manhattan Island and several miles from the main Coney Island subway repair shops in the Gravesend section of Brooklyn. Enter the South Brooklyn Railway which was constructed to convey this material to the shops as well as operate a common carrier freight system delivering and receiving carload freight from the numerous industries that dotted the Brooklyn landscape. The company even operated a package express service. The electrified line used a combination of overhead trolley wire and third rail power depending upon the locale where the trains were operating.

The northern end of the route was at the Bush Terminal where it interchanged with the Bush Terminal Railroad, one of the earliest proponents of diesel locomotives. The line operated in a southeasterly direction, sharing tracks with the PCC cars on the Church Avenue line briefly in the area of 39th Street and 2nd Avenue. At a place called Kensington Junction, the line joined another PCC line on McDonald Avenue. The South Brooklyn ran beneath the elevated to Avenue Z, where there was a yard for deliveries to the NYCTA's shops.

There were nine electric locomotives rostered over the years. Numbers 1 to 4 were built in the Company Shops between 1904 and 1907. Number 5 was built by General Electric in 1910, and numbers 6 and 7, also GE products were built in 1914. The first numbers 6 and 7 were sold in 1917 and eventually replaced by second numbers 6 and 7 in 1921 and 1925. Locos 6 and 7 were equipped with dual couplers at various times as their main job was drilling elevated cars from the Eastern Division into the Coney Island Shops. Regular MCB couplers were for freight during heavy traffic periods only.

Three Whitcomb diesel switchers were purchased from the U.S. Army during the latter years of electrified operation. Number 8 was purchased November 9, 1946, ex-U.S. Army 7966 built in 1943. Number 9, also an ex-Army Whitcomb, 7983, was sold in 1955 as a mining locomotive in Brighton, Michigan. Number 10 was a G.E. 70 ton locomotive and number 11 was originally built for the Grafton and Upton Railroad in Massachusetts, then sold in 1954 to the Claremont and Concord. It was acquired by the South Brooklyn in 1960. Electrified operation was discontinued some time in 1959. Diesel number 13 was a 1946 G.E. 70 tonner built for the Saratoga and Schuylerville in New York State. In 1947 it went to the Claremont & Concord in New Hampshire who operated it on fellow Pinsley line, Hoosac Tunnel and Wilmington R.R., as their number 23. It too came to South Brooklyn in November 1960.

In 1975, new diesel locomotives were purchased, again from GE, that continue in operation to this day. The photos on these pages were all taken in the 1955-59 era when the line shared trackage with the Brooklyn streetcars.

■ ■ ■

Box cab electric locomotive number 4 was built by the Brooklyn Heights R.R. Company in 1907 and was still performing yeoman duty on the Brooklyn waterfront at 3rd Avenue and 38th Street on April 3, 1959, a full two years after the streetcar system had been abandoned. The locomotive is now at the Shore Line Museum in Connecticut, awaiting restoration work.
(Joseph P. Saitta, Bill Volkmer Collection)

South Brooklyn G.E. steeple cab locomotive number 5 is seen at the Bush Terminal, on October 12, 1959. The design was fairly typical of dozens of G.E. locos built for interurban lines throughout the country at a time when freight traffic was become the principal revenue generator for the lines.
(Joseph P. Saitta, Bill Volkmer Collection)

(Above) Motor number 6 is operating on McDonald Avenue at Avenue Z yard on October 24, 1956. Streetcar service would end one week later over these tracks, making them freight only from that time onward. *(Frank Pfhuler)*

(Below) Here is a view of the South Brooklyn Railway Yard at 9th Avenue and 37th Street taken on September 27, 1953. Rail crane 3055 keeps company with an old Twin Coach bus that appears to have been converted to maintenance service. *(Edward S. Miller)*

113

Work Equipment

The South Brooklyn yards was apparently a repository for miscellaneous streetcar system work equipment during the latter days operation in Brooklyn. Shown on this page are three work cars of varying descriptions, all taken on March 19, 1955.

Line car 9913. *(Frank Pfhuler)*

Crane Car 9133. *(Frank Pfhuler)*

Work flat car 9220. *(Frank Pfhuler)*

South Brooklyn Railway

Sweeper 9904 was an ex-Eastern Massachusetts Street Railway work car. It was photographed at Fresh Pond Depot on March 14, 1948.
(Lawson K. Hill, Boston Chapter, NRHS Collection)

When the city of New York took over the transit operations in Brooklyn, they, for some reason, required that active work equipment be renumbered out of the 9000 series and into one or two-digit numbers. Snowplow 69 was pulled out of the Ninth Avenue Depot on October 27, 1956 for photos. Sister car 68 would later be preserved at the Shore Line Trolley Museum in Connecticut.
(Frank Pfuhler)

McGuire Cummings sweeper number 6 is being inspected one last time on October 27, 1956 at the Ninth Avenue Depot. *(Frank Pfuhler)*

South Brooklyn Railway

115

4

The Queensborough Bridge Railway

The Queensborough Bridge over Manhattan's East River was opened in 1909 and from its inception it was designed to primarily transport people in public transit vehicles. In addition to two upper level elevated tracks upstairs (2nd Avenue El), there were four streetcar tracks on the bridge. The wired tracks on the "shelf" also had conduit to accomodate Third Avenue cars from the 42nd Street line, while the inside tracks were wired-only (i.e. no conduit) and were used by the New York and Queens cars to Flushing. All wired tracks merged to enter the underground terminal on the Manhattan end after the conduit tracks left the bridge approach. The Manhattan-bound 42nd Street cars went via 60th Street to 2nd Ave., then 59th Street to 3rd Ave., using 3rd Avenue to 42nd St. continuing on to the end of the line at 12th Avenue and 42nd Street.

For the return trip (eastbound) the cars turned north on 3rd Avenue to 59th Street, then at the far side of 2nd Avenue swung onto the bridge approach. After 42nd Street service ended, the Manhattan bound trackage was removed, and the 59th Street connector was modified, de-electrified and became, in effect, a crossover with trailing point switches, connected to the Queens-bound track and the westbound 59th Street track. All un-needed conduit track in Manhattan was removed.

In order to get the cars over the unelectrified track, TARS "Emergency" trucks, large Bulldog Macks, did the honors of bringing cars from the shops for service, usually at night or during slack traffic hours. With the closure of the TARS 65th St. main shop in 1947, this practice ended and newer "Electromobiles" from New Bedford, Mass. replaced the remaining ex-Steinway, ex-Third Avenue Railway cars 531-536 over the bridge.

Between 1909 and 1922 there were four separate companies operating streetcars over the bridge: First, the Third Avenue Railway System obtained a ten-year franchise to operate over the new span as far as Queens Plaza, where two conduit loops were built. This service lasted from 1912 to 1922, but the franchise was not renewed, due to the dwindling patronage at the time. Second, the New York and Queens County Railway, operating streetcars to Flushing. Third, the Steinway lines, which served the local streets of Long Island City, Astoria, and the Pennsylvania Railroad's Sunnyside Coach Yard. That company derived its name from Steinway Piano Company, a local piano manufacturing firm. On April 27, 1922, the courts ordered the Steinway Lines to be separated from the New York and Queens. The Steinway Railway Company assumed operation of the lines over the Queensborough Bridge as a result. Cars of the New York and Queens from Flushing terminated at Long Island City and did not enter Manhattan.

Last but not least, the Manhattan and Queens Traction Company, operated one long car route through Jamaica on Sutphin Blvd., terminating at 109th Ave. It was popularly known as "The Queens Blvd. trolley", the only venue in Queens with two fare-zones on the cars.

The original four tracks over the bridge carried the New York and Queens County Railway cars just inside the bridge girders, but in the roadway, while the other three companies, including the conduit-powered Third Ave. cars hugged the outside of the bridge on a shelf like arrangement. From 1913 to 1916, the New York and Queens County Railway used the two inner tracks, but opted to put their cars out on the outside shelf, in 1916. This track was shared with the Manhattan and Queens, but they did not share power. Rather, there were two individual trolley wires with an insulator placed between them (the M&Q having their own wire). All cars crossing the bridge after 1916 used the "shelf". The four tracks were narrowed down to two in 1922 when the Third Avenue discontinued service over the bridge. This allowed the Steinway Lines to move over onto the outside of the bridge and provided more room for autos and taxis, not to mention trucks and buses, on the bridge.

Over the years the subways began carrying the bulk of the passenger traffic and streetcars became less important. The Steinway Street and 31st Street lines, plus the Manhattan and Queens continued to cross the bridge until 1937, when the M&Q gave way to buses. Then in 1939, the Steinway Lines motorized all of their lines on the Island. A problem then arose because there was no way for buses to serve the hospital on Welfare Island in the center of the East River, which the bridge spanned. The trolleys stopped at a small station with an elevator on the northern side of the bridge to take folks and vehicles down to the street level. There was a similar stop on the Long Island City end of the bridge at Vernon Boulevard, but for pedestrians only. So the trolleys in some form needed to be kept running. Enter the Queensborough Bridge Railway.

The Queensborough Bridge Railway utilized old Steinway wooden cars, originally Manhattan Bridge 3-cent line, from 1939 until 1949. In 1939 the TARS 65th Street shops rebuilt and overhauled cars 531-536 for further service on the bridge, the remainder being scrapped (some renumbering took place). C-55 trucks replaced the Brill 39Es, which had replaced the Standard 045 maximum traction trucks the cars had when new. The Brill 39E trucks had only one powered axle per truck (Maximum Traction?) and were not good at climbing the bridge inclines. In 1949 secondhand Osgood Bradley Electromobiles were purchased from the now defunct Union Street Railway in New Bedford, Mass. These cars were totally isolated from the outside streetcar world, so they were maintained over a pit at the 2nd Avenue and 59th Street terminal, under Manhattan. During operation, the cars only changed ends once during each round trip. At the Manhattan end there was an underground loop for turning the cars, whereas at the Long Island City end, the operator was required to move the controls from one end of the car to the other. The last day of revenue service on the Queensborough Bridge Railway was April 7, 1957 with the final pole on a New York state streetcar being pulled early in the morning of April 8th that is until the Buffalo light rail line opened in the 1980s.

(Left) Former Union Street Railway car 603, built by Osgood Bradley in 1930, was pressed into Queensborough service before being repainted into the Steinway Lines bus orange and cream scheme. It is seen here at Queens Plaza probably around 1949. The cars retained their New Bedford, MA numbers after repainting in New York.
(Eugene Van Dusen)

(Below) About eight years later, in April 1957, car 605 had not only been repainted, but had collected its share of New York City dirt and grime without benefit of a good washing. No need to wash it, it was headed to the scrap heap shortly. *(Al Holtz)*

Car 605 rolls to a stop at the Welfare Island intermediate station. Manhattan can be seen in the background on this hot summer's day, August 22, 1954. *(Charles Ballard)*

Osgood Bradley Electromobile 602 is eastbound towards Queens Plaza. Long Island City is in the background in this April 21, 1956 view. *(Edward S. Miller)*

In early afternoon sun, this photo illustrates the relationship of the trackway to the roadway on the Queensborough Bridge. 603 is at the Welfare Island stop on October 4, 1953. *(Eugene Van Dusen)*

(Above) At one of the few points on the line where the cars poked out into the sunshine, the operator has apparently stopped the car for the benefit of the photographer. The location is near the eastern end of the line approaching Queens Plaza and the date was September 15, 1956.
(Lawson K. Hill, Boston Chapter, NRHS Collection)

(Above) Early morning sun was best to photograph the cars at the turnback point in Queens Plaza. Car 607 was still in pretty decent shape on July 12, 1952 after about three years of New York service. *(James J. Buckley, P. Allen Copeland Collection)*

(Right) A late winter storm has dropped a layer of snow through the cracks of the elevated tracks above at Queens Plaza – 28th Street. Car 606 is eastbound headed back to Manhattan on March 17, 1956. *(Frank Pfuhler)*

(Left) On May 20, 1951 car 605 the operator has already put up the rear pole and pulled down the front pole at the Queens Plaza terminal. This ritual was performed several times in an eight hour shift because it only took about ten minutes to make a one-way trip over the bridge. These 1930 model cars were pretty much the state-of-the-art in streetcar construction for their time, but the design was obviously superceded by the PCC cars in later years and not replicated. Builder Osgood-Bradley, of Worcester, Mass. became Pullman-Standard during the PCC car era.
(Eugene Van Dusen)

The 601 is leaving the terminal on the east side of the river on July 3, 1955. The driver of the new T-bird in the background was probably more interested in his wheels than those of the streetcar. *(Frank Pfuhler)*

The location of this photo was about the longest stretch of street running on the line where unobstructed photos could be shot. Car 601 is westbound on August 22, 1954.
(Charles Ballard)

A BMT subway train passes a group of railfans who are photographing car 602 on February 23, 1957. The car and the subway train will soon disappear underground under Manhattan streets. One of the fans appears to have put a New Bedford destination sign in place for the photo.
(Frank Pfuhler)

Just prior to entering the subterranean terminal on the Manhattan end of the bridge, car 602 does a traffic-defying twist that required a certain amount of visual dexterity on the part of the trolley operator. The photo was made on July 3, 1955. And, FYI, that jog in the track headed for the underground terminal was left over from the days when there were two tracks coming off the bridge. The shelf track with conduit and wire headed for 60th St. and the roadway track went directly into the hole. So that pole cars from the shelf could get to the hole, a crossover was in place for that purpose and that jog remained while all other track was removed. A similar situation existed on the Queens-bound side, but the track rebuilding made for a gentler access to the shelf.
(Frank Pfuhler)

■■■ Preserved Cars of New York City ■■■

Several New York area trolleys have been preserved, some to a greater extent of preservation than others insofar as their degree of restoration is concerned. Here we shall take a closeup look at a few of them. The preserved cars are divided between the Shore Line Trolley Museum in Branford, Connecticut, the Connecticut Electric Railway in Warehouse Point, and the Trolley Museum of New York, in Kingston, NY.

(Right) Former Pay Car 2 is seen at the Garden Ave. yards in Mt. Vernon in 1947. In an earlier time, the employees were paid in cash and cars such as this that had been converted from regular passenger service to rolling banks were utilized to go around to the various carbarns on payday and distribute pay envelopes to operating and maintenance employees alike. Car 2 exactly like Pay Car 1, was scrapped in the big cleanup of everything not saleable in 1947 & '48. Both were in dead storage in the Amsterdam Av. carhouse in 1942 when Vitaly Uzoff wanted an "ERA" car. The very friendly shopmen advised Uzoff to pick #1 as the #2 was bad order for some reason. So he boldly asked Supt. Frank Seeney to have the car moved up to Garden Ave. and it was. Before Uzoff was discharged from the Army (and going into the Reserves), Ron Parente discovered the "ERA #1" and asked if the car was for sale. Supt. Seeney said he could have it for $100. So Ron borrowed from his father who had to sign the bill of sale as Ron was under age. His father warned him that he had to restore the car or he'd charge him interest. His father lived to age 94, so he saw the car completely restored, as Union Railway 316 which runs perfectly well on occasion at the Branford trolley museum. It was donated to BERA but to me, it will always be "Ron's car."
(Caption by Karl Groh, Frank Pfuhler Collection)

(Above) Branford, Connecticut is now home to this gem. This photo was made August 4, 1949 shortly after the car's arrival in Branford. *(Eugene Van Dusen)*

(Above) Third Avenue Railway car 629 was sold to Vienna, Austria where it operated as number 4239 for several years. It was ultimately shipped back to the U.S., becoming the property of the Shore Line Trolley Museum in Connecticut. Fully restored, it was photographed in September 1996.
(Bill Volkmer Collection)

Car 4573 is shown here in its closed configuration on Island Ave. near East 71st St. The was on the Flatbush Ave. line, on the Everett White private excursion, October 10, 1948. *(Everett A. White, courtesy of Don Harold)*

Convertible car 4550 was used as a work car for many years and was not in nearly as good condition as sister car 4573. Like 4573, it was built in 1906 by Jewett as a four-motor convertible and spent its last days as a tow car probably out of Flatbush Depot. After abandonment, the car was sold to a private owner put on display in South Carver, MA. Following the demise of the Edaville operation, it was sold to the City of Detroit but stored in Pennsylvania for rebuilding. When the Detroit trolley line failed to materialize, the aging carbody fell upon hard times. It ultimately found its way to Station Square in Pittsburgh where it was partially restored. Since the car had no Pittsburgh significance, it was traded to the Middletown and Hummellstown Railroad, where it resides today.

Former tow-car 4550 is operating on a fantrip on Coney Island Ave. overpass crossing the Belt Parkway. Brown livery was B&QT's way of identifying non-revenue equipment. The date of the fantrip was May 26, 1951. *(Everett A. White, courtesy of Donald Harold)*

Brooklyn car 4573 was built by Jewett in 1906 as a double end, four-motor, open platform, two-man convertible. It ran continuously in passenger service until the one-man era forced it into non-revenue use as a tow car, assigned to the 58th Street Depot. Towards the end of streetcar operation, the fans discovered the car to be in good condition and requested the use of same on a fantrip. The initial request was denied but some political "string pulling" on the part of some of the more influential railfans managed to persuade the management to allow the car to take part in a ceremony commemorating the 1898 unification of the five boroughs into New York City in 1898. Thus, on August 22, 1948, (the day after streetcar service ended in the Bronx) a carload of "celebrants", mostly railfans departed the Park Row terminal for a tour of many of the remaining Brooklyn streetcar lines. A second trip was operated October 3, 1948 to cover those lines not covered in the first trip, but minus the banners. Both trips were sponsored by the Branford Electric Railway Association and profits helped to pay for the car's eventual shipment to Connecticut. A third trip was run on October 10, 1948 by Everett White with the car in a closed configuration. Soon thereafter the car was moved to Branford where it was restored to its original passenger carrying configuration.

Work car 4550 was pulled out of the Ninth Avenue depot for photos on September 27, 1953. At that time it had not been earmarked for preservation. *(Edward S. Miller)*

Third Avenue Railway 220, now operating at the Shore Line Trolley Museum, East Haven, Connecticut, is the last surviving New York City cable car. As such, it was built in 1893 as number 20. The cables were removed from the underground conduits and twin contact rails were installed to provide electricity to the cars. The car was motorized in 1899 and renumbered 220. Then in 1908, the car was relegated to work car service as a slot scraper numbered 33, a number it retained until the demise of the Manhattan conduit rail lines in 1947. In 1948, the car was moved to Branford for restoration as a passenger railcar, albeit modified for trolley pole operation. The photo above was taken at Branford on September 5, 1948 while the photo below shows the restoration complete in 1996.

(top, Eugene Van Dusen; bottom, Bill Volkmer Collection)